THE P
STANFORD

published by the
Stanford Alumni Association

THE GORBACHEV ERA

**Edited by Alexander Dallin
and Condoleezza Rice**

Stanford Alumni Association
Stanford, California

THE PORTABLE STANFORD is a series
publication of the Stanford Alumni Association. Each book is an original work
written expressly for this series by a
member of the Stanford University fac-
ulty. The PS series is designed to bring
the widest possible sampling of Stanford's intellectual resources into the
homes of alumni. It includes books based
on current research as well as books that
deal with philosophical issues, which by
their nature reflect to a greater degree the
personal views of their authors.

THE PORTABLE STANFORD
Stanford Alumni Association
Bowman Alumni House
Stanford, California 94305

Library of Congress Catalog Card
Number 85-063731
ISBN: 0-916318-17-8
ISBN: 0-916318-18-8 pbk.

El Lissitzky, *1919*

Preface   **vii**

1 **The Legacy of the Past**   **1**
Alexander Dallin

2 **The Nature of Soviet Politics and
the Gorbachev Leadership**   **11**
George W. Breslauer

3 **Soviet Society in Transition**   **31**
Gail W. Lapidus

4 **Problems Facing the Soviet Economy**   **43**
Marie Lavigne

5 **Science and Technology in the Soviet Union:
Historical Background and Contemporary Problems**   **61**
Kendall E. Bailes

6 **The Soviet Nationality Question**   **73**
Gail W. Lapidus

7 **A Writer Meets the State:
Literary Authorship in Modern Russia**   **85**
Gregory Freidin

CONTENTS

8   **Dissent in the Soviet Union**   95
Robert Conquest

9   **Civil-Military Relations in the Mid-1980s**   107
Timothy J. Colton

10   **The Development of Soviet Military Power**   121
Condoleezza Rice

11   **Arms Control is Back in the Soviet Union: Where is it Going?**   139
Coit D. Blacker

12   **The Soviet Alliance System**   155
Condoleezza Rice

13   **A Soviet Master Plan? The Non-Existent "Grand Design" in World Affairs**   167
Alexander Dallin

Recommended Reading   179

The Authors   181

Credits   183

PREFACE

When the Stanford Alumni Association first asked us to develop a series of lectures on the Soviet Union, Konstantin Chernenko was General Secretary of the Communist Party, Dmitri Ustinov was Minister of Defense, and Andrei Gromyko was Foreign Minister. These were people who had occupied leadership positions in the Soviet Union for a generation or more. One of our first thoughts was how to handle the imminent succession and the problems and opportunities it was bound to create. The Kremlin leadership had changed hands twice in two years, and specialists on the Soviet Union were playing a waiting game in anticipation of Chernenko's demise.

By the time the lectures on which the essays in this book are based were presented, all three men were out of power: Chernenko and Ustinov were dead, and Gromyko had been "promoted" to a largely ceremonial post in the Soviet government. The long-awaited generational shift was finally well under way. Suffice it to note that Mikhail Gorbachev, the new General Secretary of the Communist Party of the Soviet Union, had been a Party member for only four years when Gromyko became Foreign Minister. As of the 27th Party Congress in February 1986, the average age of the Politburo's members is almost fifteen years less than that of its predecessors.

This is therefore a propitious and an important time to take a look at the Soviet Union with fresh eyes. We have become accustomed to seeing in Moscow an overly bureaucratized and slow moving government run by elderly men. Those men are now gone. Whether this portends rapid or moderate change—significant or cosmetic—or a mere reshuffling to be followed by business as usual remains to be seen. Change, moreover, need not mean change for the better—either for the Soviet population or for us. A different Soviet Union will not necessarily be more humane at home or less troublesome abroad. But we know that the new Soviet leadership believes that change must come to the Soviet Union. Of course, this will be a change *within* the system and not a change *of* the Soviet system; this in itself, however, is no reason to dismiss it in advance as insignificant.

In first drawing up and now tackling the agenda for change, Gorbachev faces a formidable accumulation of problems that are bound to tax his and his associates' seemingly boundless energy and professed willingness to innovate. Economic stagnation, along with widespread inefficiency, mismanagement, corruption, and a lack of incentives to do better—all these threaten not only economic growth but perhaps also the Soviet Union's social and military well-being. There are simply not enough resources to allocate for investment, consumption, and defense at levels that would satisfy the experts, the politicians, and the diverse interests in Soviet politics and society. No doubt structural and operational reforms within an economic and administrative system whose origin was in the breakneck industrialization drive of the 1930s are needed to make better use of human, managerial, and natural resources, and to take advantage of the technological revolution that has already occurred in the West and in Japan. Yet inertia and the new leadership's fear of change and destabilization stand in the way of change, and there are difficult technical problems and political choices to be made. Chief among the trade-offs is the risk that greater initiative and flexibility in the system through decentralization might well come only at the expense of political control.

There have also been hints of a crisis of confidence in Soviet society. Youth, even when loyal, often lack enthusiasm and dedication; the creative artist once again tends to assume the role of a subtle critic; alcoholism and labor discipline are only two among many salient problems; and the Party appears to lack real answers—other than tired stereotypes—for the many questions it needs to face.

These domestic problems have come to the fore at a time when there are new challenges to Soviet power abroad. Thirty years ago the Soviet Union was a regional power; today, as one of two global superpowers, it is struggling to hang on to its central role in world affairs. It is faced with a renewed military and technological challenge from the United States at a time when economic stringency might dictate a course of less intensive devotion of resources to its weapons program.

Eastern Europe, the backbone of the Soviet security system, is a source of continual concern, with troubling—though very different— tensions in Poland and Czechoslovakia and increasingly independent regimes in Hungary and Romania. To a Soviet leadership presently bogged down in guerrilla warfare in Afghanistan the gains of "socialism," Soviet-style, in the Third World must also appear less solid, less worthwhile, and more costly than they did just ten years ago. And the superpower relationship—at least until the "summit" at Geneva—continues to be uncertain at best.

We have tried in this series of essays to discuss some of the key dimensions of the Soviet Union and the problems on its agenda. It is important that we neither brush off these problems as trivial nor assume that they are so severe that the system is on the verge of collapse. This book, based on a limited number of lectures, does not pretend to offer a comprehensive treatment. A number of topics— for instance, the role of religion, the place of important institutions such as the KGB (Secret Police), and Gosplan (State Planning Commission), and many aspects of foreign affairs—are not systematically discussed. But we believe that the issues covered here are central to an understanding of the Soviet Union today.

We do not attempt to predict but rather seek to describe, as clearly and simply as we can, the setting, the leadership, the economy, the society, the military, as well as such outstanding issues as arms control, the nationalities, and the Soviet alliance system. Taken together, these lectures should provide the background for a better understanding of the fascinating events that are likely to take place in the Soviet Union in the years to come. That was our intention when we planned the lectures that brought our authors together, in the summer of 1985, for the Stanford Summer College. We were fortunate in securing the participation of some of the most able and best informed specialists on the Soviet Union. The response to their lectures encouraged us to offer them in this form to a wider public. We have intentionally kept them in the style in which they were delivered, without requiring scholarly documentation, cross-references, or cautionary reservations at every step.

The Editors

Stanford, California
January 1986

El Lissitzky, *1920*

THE LEGACY OF THE PAST

El Lissitzky, "Proletariat," 1925

ALEXANDER DALLIN

1

Environment and heredity: Each has played a part in shaping the present Soviet Union. And since all the essays that follow deal with the present environment, let us here take a brief look at the impact of heredity—the legacy of the past.

What we want to know, in effect, is (in the nonsensical words of a book title of some years ago), "Why they behave like Russians." We can make mercifully short shrift of some of the many "explanations" that have been proposed. Some writers have attributed all that is characteristically Russian to the climate and geography. But the simple fact is that North America has plains as vast, and Canada has long stretches as cold and forbidding, as Russia's. Yet neither has generated the same kind of political system or attitudes that we find in the USSR. Let's beware of simple answers.

There used to be another theory that, in their attitudes toward authority, Russians were perenially torn between submission and anarchy. At one time anthropologists like Geoffrey Gorer took this very seriously, attributing it all to the tight swaddling of Russian babies, and thus giving rise to a theory dismissed by its detractors as "diaperology." I recall that in the fifties one of our more prominent colleagues, then still a mere graduate student at Harvard, used to recite a little verse:

"Little Ivan, swaddled tight,
Can't turn left and can't turn right.
Hence the mighty Russian nation
Tolerates no deviation."

This was not only terrible poetry but also poor social science. It turned out that other scholars had found the same tension between obedience and revolt in Ireland and Mexico, in Bengal India and in Spain, and in many other places where there is no swaddling.

There are plenty of other pet theories offered as master keys to Soviet belief and behavior. Among these, history is bound to have a central place: the image of the Soviet system as a product of Russia's past. What about it?

We are all captives of our past, real or imaginary; all peoples live by myths and collective memories, accurate or inaccurate. That is true of the Soviet Union too, but which past, in fact, are we talking about? One visitor came back from the Soviet Union with the astute observation that the country was living simultaneously in every century from the thirteenth to the twenty-first.

A friend tells of driving by the National Archives in Washington one day and asking the taxi driver what the inscription over its portals, "The past is prologue," meant. "Mister," the cabbie replied, "that means, 'You ain't seen nothin' yet.'" What then does the prologue say to us? Historians divide. There are those who will tell us of a thousand years of Muscovite autocracy, serfdom, poverty, brutality, and backwardness in Russia; the influence of the Byzantine tradition on the Russian church; and the impact of the Mongols and Tatars on the lives and institutions of the peoples of Russia when they ruled the Eurasian plain. They will stress the failure of Russia to experience the Renaissance and the Reformation; they'll recount the precedents that Ivan the Terrible and Peter the Great ostensibly provided for Comrade Dzhugashvili, whom we know as Joseph Stalin; they'll recite the lack of individual freedoms and civil rights; they'll document the frequent hostility of Russians to foreigners; and they will stress the centuries of uncomprehending polarization between rulers and ruled. And most of this is quite true.

And then we ask ourselves what we know of the Soviet Union. We remember the beautiful pictures of the Russian countryside and the old churches and estates. We think of the Russian ballet and its tradition, from *Swan Lake* to *Spartacus*; we recall the powerful themes of Russian music, now majestic, now haunting, from Tchaikovsky to Shostakovich; and we lose ourselves in the captivating, interminable novels of Tolstoy and Dostoyevsky, in the prose and poetry of Russian authors whose subtlety, complexity, sensitivity we had never fathomed—and we realize that there was, there must have been, another Russia than that of the Cossacks on horseback chasing the starving peasants, or of the idle gentry, an ignorant church, and a corrupt police; or a state used to dealing with others only by the use of force. We think of the many times Russia not only attacked but was invaded from abroad, and we wonder to what extent hostility to outsiders was not then a natural thing.

If there was (let us call it) a Slavophile tradition that stressed and cherished the distinctiveness of Russia, there were also the Westernizers who saw salvation in modernization. For every "tradition" we can find a counter-tradition; for every Dostoyevsky there was a Turgenev. And if an anti-Western, authoritarian animus runs like a red thread from Patriarch Nikon through Berdiaev to Solzhenitsyn, the opposite thread links (in fact or in myth and symbol) ancient Novgorod and its popular assembly; liberals like Pavel Miliukov, the Constituent Assembly of 1918, and the saintly Andrei Sakharov. Before the twentieth century, institutionalized pluralism in Russian political life was indeed hard to detect, but the emergence of political parties, partisan newspapers and journals, and the vigorous public life—along with the cultural elan and economic development—toward the end of the monarchy, before World War I, testify to the fact that the gap between Russia and the more developed countries had at last begun to shrink.

Let us remember then that there are strikingly different traditions, even contradictory ones, in the Russian past, which compete for a piece of the present.

Of course there are important continuities in Russian (as in all other) history. They may be strongest in social and economic history, easiest to trace in regard to popular values and attitudes. Attitudes toward authority and the state are one likely candidate for significant continuity. The almost unquestioning acceptance by many Russians of a powerful centralized state, while far from unique, does contrast sharply with the characteristic American suspicion of regulation, government, and politicians. The role of the state as principal source and instrument of change, as well as its paternalistic function as dispenser of welfare, almost universally accepted in the Soviet Union (and even by emigrés from the USSR), have their "objective" historical causes. The paucity of voluntary associations, organizations mediating between state and individual, has been remarked upon more than once.

Even if much of this had begun to change before the Revolution of 1917, it is another part of the legacy left to the Bolshevik era. The weakness of individualism, the frailty of representative institutions at the national level, the absence of the values and forms of the rule of law—here are but a few of the prerevolutionary trends that have indeed affected the Soviet era. Undoubtedly prejudices, stereotypes, and customs of all sorts have persisted as well. And there are memories and myths relating to the many foreign invasions and incursions that, in the past, exposed Russia to attack from abroad—and with them goes some popular determination not to let such experiences be repeated.

The question is what weight to attach to such items. The fear of foreign attack can readily be manipulated by unscrupulous leaders. Even if their attribution is valid, many of the traits cited above are by no means unique to Russia. The love/hate attitude toward the "advanced" West is none too different from the ambivalence toward the "First World" found in India, Nigeria, or Japan. Many aspects of the Soviet hostility to "bourgeois" norms and values seem to resemble those found both among the aristocracy and in slums the world over. The personalized attachment to the ruler is a common trait in less developed societies. Autocracy, bureaucracy, red tape, and military necessity have many analogs across time and space.

There are also the conditions under which Lenin & Co. had to function as virtual outlaws under the old regime. These made the acceptance of violence and secrecy second nature, and they reinforced the endemic suspicion of spontaneity, promoting instead the characteristic Bolshevik stress on discipline and organization. There are no doubt other habits and norms that have been perpetuated and internalized by the population. In fact, the Soviet regime in the 1930s and 1940s came to recognize the depth of such attachment to traditional symbols and heroes and worked to capitalize on them, as indeed it succeeded in doing most tellingly during the "Great Fatherland War" (a label Lenin would have scorned), when the victorious prerevolutionary past, from Alexander Nevsky to tsarist field marshals, was again glorified and extolled. Without a doubt, national pride (along with national insecurity) is a strong and widespread sentiment in the Soviet Union today, and that includes a (selective) identification with the nation's past.

No less important, however, is the fact that many features of the Soviet experience had no prerevolutionary Russian analogs or precedents. Marxism, adapted to Russian conditions by Lenin, was for better or for worse, a product of Western European thought. The federal structure of the Soviet state, the emancipation of women, the destruction of the old propertied classes, the network of closely controlled communist parties abroad, and the renunciation of tsarist treaties and foreign debts were only a few of the many features wherein the Soviet regime differed fundamentally from its tsarist predecessors.

The point is simple: Let us not overdo the determinism of historical continuity. Russia's past need not predetermine its future. Here let me touch on one, somewhat extreme, school of historical and political interpretation which I believe needs to be challenged and set aside. Historians must know not only the uses of history but also its limits. The future can never be assumed to be a replica, or an extrapolation, of the past; if it were, history as a subject of study would indeed be as boring as some of our students allege. To the earlier saying that "history does not repeat itself; historians do," one might add the remark of Sidney Hook that "those who always remember the past often don't know when it's over." One could argue that there is no more validity in historical determinism than in economic or technological determinism; no more in regard to Russia than in respect to other countries.

Let us assume for the moment that the image of Russia as offered in the so-called "hard-line historiography" (the apt term is James Cracraft's) is substantially accurate—essentially, Russian history as the image of a brutal, boorish country, ruled by force and possessed by a relentless drive to expand abroad; combining cunning and suspicion, intolerance and xenophobia.

Whatever the particular traits of a given society, the process of socioeconomic modernization tends to lessen the specific weight and the saliency of traditional culture. "Development" is typically marked by the uprooting of large groups from their traditional environment in the course of wholesale urbanization, and accompanied by a change of occupations and of reference groups, by greater exposure to mass communications and access to new sources of information, greater interaction with the world abroad, and an attenuation of traditional attachments. If this is so, then we might expect those traditional values and norms, that traditional culture, to have been substantially weakened precisely, and paradoxically, in the process of the transformation that the Soviet regime brought about at such a tremendous cost—one of the many unintended consequences of Soviet rule.

Do we need to invoke the Tatars, the Time of Troubles, Muscovite obscurantists of centuries past, or the "Black Hundred" to understand current Soviet behavior and attitudes? It is generally a sound rule to opt first of all for simplicity in explaining causality rather than for the more devious, remote, complex, or overdetermined alternatives. Indeed, in regard to other societies, this is normally done without much dispute. Who would refer to Savonarola, Cromwell, or Robespierre, to the War of the Roses, or to the Huguenots, if you sought to explain the contemporary behavior of the Italians, British, or French? And while there may well be a traditional component, say, in the Soviet inclination toward "excessive" secrecy, there are also perfectly rational explanations for why Stalin (or his successors) chose to conceal much of what was going on in the USSR from foreign eyes and ears.

All these injunctions together argue that, even if we were to accept the accuracy of the "hard-line" determinists' account of Russian history, we would be well advised to guard against a mindless extrapolation from the past into the future. With a similar deterministic bias, a Parisian in the 1780s—prior to the capture of the Bastille—would have argued that French political culture was absolutist and authoritarian and permitted no republican or democratic traits. Political scientists and journalists writing about Germany and Japan, prior to 1945, did indeed often—and erroneously—deny the possibility of any significant change in political behavior and institutions, given the dominant and presumably persistent political cultures in these two countries. It behooves us then to allow for some doubt and humility in our projections and to beware of erecting a mental wall against the possibility of future change.

Actually there is much to question concerning the factual and analytical accuracy of the version of Russian history propounded by the continuity school. Regrettably, we can touch on only a few relevant points here.

One is the utility of comparative history. At different times a number of trends similar to those found in Russia could be detected elsewhere—in Prussia or Japan or the rest of Eastern Europe, or in regard to the conquest of vast spaces in Northern Asia, even in the American westward advance of the frontier. The revolutions of 1917, too, can be fruitfully examined within the framework of comparative history. We discover that a good deal of the alleged Russian uniqueness fades once the Russian experience is compared with that of other societies. Thus—citing almost at random—J.H. Plumb reminds us that in the seventeenth century even Englishmen "killed, tortured, and executed each other for political beliefs; they sacked towns and brutalized the countryside. They were subjected to conspiracy, plot, and invasion." It would be easy to document the brutality of the Thirty Years' War or the insensitivity of Europe's crowned heads to popular aspirations. As for the misery of the countryside, prior to modernization and the emergence of a sense of citizenship, we need go no further than Eugen Weber's description in *Peasants into Frenchmen*.

India and Japan, like Russia, failed to experience the Renaissance, but without therefore turning to Bolshevism. Tsarist officialdom deserves careful comparison with others, such as the Prussian or the Swedish. Serfdom, autocracy, a service nobility, and borrowing from more technologically advanced societies—none of these was peculiarly Russian. And if in the end the autocracy decayed in St. Petersburg, so did it in the Ottoman Empire, and under the Habsburgs and Hohenzollerns too. True, much of what developed in Russia came after a substantial time lag and often had a particular Russian stamp to it. There is truth in Henry L. Roberts' formula that, by comparison with the European West, Russia often seemed both "related and belated"—but assuredly not unique.

Perhaps the area in which the continuity thesis has been applied with greatest abandon is that of Russian (and Soviet) foreign policy. It is interesting, of course, that Poland, Finland, Manchuria, and Northern Iran were the targets of expansionist drives both before and after 1917. But what this similarity in the locus of Russian expansion illustrates is the "continuity of geography." It says nothing about the continuity of interests or objectives. To be sure, a recital of tsarist and Soviet interest in neighboring territories, from the Balkans to Korea, prompts questions regarding similarities. But a closer look, I believe, is bound to lead to the conclusion that not only the international context but also the definition of interests and objectives, the self-image, and the sense of one's own—and one's adversaries'—capabilities have (for good reasons) radically changed over the last century.

The discontinuity of objectives is particularly clear in regard to the Middle East. While in the nineteenth century the tsar's court was concerned to keep the Holy Places out of the hands of the infidels, the Soviet authorities can hardly be said to have shared *this* worry. A century ago Russian interest in controlling the Straits was in significant measure the result of St. Petersburg's wish to assure the safety of Russian grain exports to the West as they traveled from Black Sea ports to the Mediterranean. Today Moscow looks back with nostalgia upon an era in which Russia had grain to spare for export abroad.

The point of all this is of course neither to argue that there have not been significant similarities and continuities over time, nor to claim that there were no significant differences between Russian and other foreign policies. The question is whether the burden of these constants outweighs the impact of change, and whether these differences between Russia and other societies were so fundamental and enduring as to set it up as unique and essentially beyond the prospect of repair. Here the answer must be a plain "no."

Finally, a word about the legacy of the Soviet experience. The Soviet system has, after all, endured for the major part of this century. Many of the institutions invented by the Bolsheviks—beginning with the soviets themselves as the units of government—have remained. In political education and indoctrination there is an almost ritual stress on continuity and on reference to the Leninist past for the regime's authority and legitimacy. I am convinced that Soviet leaders do themselves a disservice by forever denying that they have departed from the orthodox path charted by the Bolshevik "classics," that is, by refusing to acknowledge all change. For, in fact, their world view, their mind-set, their expectations and priorities have significantly changed since 1917. How could they fail to do so? This is not the place to discuss the continuing functions and the diminishing role of Leninist ideology and the myths that go with it. But as the generations that provide the leaders of the Soviet state have changed—and are changing—and as their formative experiences change, it is important to bear in mind that both Soviet leadership and Soviet society operate within a variety of constraints. Some of these are imposed by the international environment, some are indeed rooted in their past, and some are defined by internal factors—currently, resource and budgetary constraints, contending interests among the Soviet elite, scientific and technological limitations, problems of civic morale and legitimacy, and others that are discussed in the essays that follow.

The years since the Bolsheviks seized power in 1917 have failed to produce a "new Soviet man" (or woman), despite the promises of the Soviet leaders and the fears of their adversaries. The goals that they set for themselves then seem today more utopian than ever. But if the population is far from conforming to that communist stereotype, neither are we dealing with "tsarist Russia in overalls" (as one British observer put it). We do ourselves a serious disservice if we think of our Soviet adversaries as the "hordes of Genghis Khan with a nuclear bomb." The reality may or may not be less dramatic, but it is surely less primitive and more complex.

I have tried to suggest that there is a legacy of the Russian past, but that it is not nearly so compelling as we are sometimes told. It is dangerously misleading to start out with the notion that nothing can change in Russia, that the people are the slaves of a past they cannot escape or shed, and that every country gets the government it deserves. Things—in the USSR as elsewhere—can get better and they can get worse, and at least marginally we can affect the outcome by what we do and don't do. We are once again at a point where at least some changes are in the offing. Change is in the air, and it will be important for us to observe, to gauge, and to understand.

THE NATURE OF SOVIET POLITICS AND THE GORBACHEV LEADERSHIP

El Lissitzky, *1919*

GEORGE W. BRESLAUER

The Soviet political system, from my perspective, is a bureaucratic dictatorship, in which popular participation in decision-making processes is largely ritualized, and in which the officials in the various bureaucracies are not regularly held accountable to public constituencies or to a broader public. It is also a polity in which the public is not permitted to engage in dramatization of its demands, desires, needs, or yearnings, nor to use avenues of publicity not sanctioned in advance by officialdom, and in which political requests and demands coming from the public must be channeled through officially controlled channels.

Because of these features, I call the Soviet system a bureaucratic dictatorship—a dictatorship in that there is no real accountability to the public, and bureaucratic in that a large bureaucracy run by a huge officialdom monopolizes the game of politics.

To ask how responsive this regime is to popular sentiments is to pose a very different question. After all, you can, in principle, have a benevolent dictatorship—a dictatorship that is congruent with popular sentiment and delivers the goods in various ways, even if it is not held regularly accountable through political mechanisms such as elections, referenda, initiatives, and the like.

One could make a fairly strong case, even though it would be controversial, that in many respects the Gorbachev regime is now responsive to public sentiment in the Soviet Union. There is a cultural congruence between the policies of the regime on the one hand and a historical deference to political authority on the other hand—a historical lack of a liberal-democratic political culture. The prevailing historical consciousness tends to see the only alternative to imposed order as anarchy. Definitions of justice and equity in the popular consciousness are typically based on substantive criteria, such as "Who wins?" or "What do I get?" rather than on procedural criteria, such as "Were the rules of the game played fairly?"

In a more specific sense, certain features of regime policy must be consistent with the expectations of many, if not most, Soviet citizens. One feature of regime policy, for example, is the welfare state. The welfare state has many aspects to it: price stability on basic commodities—the price of eggs and butter is the same today as it was in 1962; job security—except for cases of gross malfeasance, most workers can't be fired from their jobs; cradle-to-grave social security, free public education, free public health, and the like.

In addition to a welfare state, the regime maintains a law-and-order state. When you consider that a large portion of the Soviet population possesses a hard-hat mentality, you can understand that a regime based on law and order is congruent with their expectations of the political system.

The Soviet Union is also a national security state, in which the ability to assure peace for forty years to a population that in the previous forty years has had so much devastation from war is a positive good in the eyes of its citizens. The regime has also achieved an international status that elicits patriotic pride, for example, in the fact that the Soviet Union, as one of two superpowers in the world today, is accorded a great deal of deference.

Finally, policy must be congruent with popular expectations of opportunity for individual advancement. This is a regime whose social policies provide opportunities for education—and with that education, upward mobility—to the masses of the population. To be sure, the opportunities for social mobility today are far fewer than they were forty or fifty years ago. Nevertheless, by the standards of an industrial society they are good, and even if they are rapidly slowing down, people's images of a structure that provides social opportunities tend to linger for a long time—even after the actual situation has changed. In other words, there is today among many, if not most, people in the Soviet Union, a Horatio Alger myth that anyone can make it in this society if one works hard, keeps one's nose clean, gets the needed education, and takes advantage of opportunities.

But the question of a regime's responsiveness is distinct from that of its political processes and from the forms of political representation and accountability that are built into that system. When I think of the phrase, "the nature of Soviet politics," what I have in mind is the nature of the political process.

To fathom the political process in the Soviet Union, it is best to think of a huge bureaucratic pyramid. At the top of that pyramid is the Politburo. The pyramid then expands outward to encompass hundreds of thousands of officials of the various bureaucracies in the country. The result is a huge hierarchy of officialdom, which seeks to manage or to supervise almost all aspects of societal, economic, and military life in the Soviet Union.

A recent article in the *San Francisco Chronicle* quoted an article in a Soviet periodical that said, "If only we could release ten percent of the chauffeurs who are assigned to Soviet officials, we could release for employment elsewhere, such as in public transport, some 60,000 first rate drivers." I don't know how much duplication there is in those figures—the same person could act as driver for several officials—but if we assume one chauffeur per official, we've got 60,000 Soviet officials right there, and there must be several layers of Soviet officialdom who do not get any drivers at all. This suggests some idea of just how many people there are in a centrally planned system that is trying to administer the economy, supervise all aspects of political and societal life, and also supervise the standard bureaucracies of order, the police and the military.

Within this bureaucratic pyramid there are many vertical bureaucracies. An economic bureaucracy, staffed by economic managers and planners, runs from the State Planning Committee in Moscow all the way down to the production unit. The governmental bureaucracy is also multilayered, with the Supreme Soviet in Moscow at the top of a structure that runs down to the smallest local village council—the local soviet. The military bureaucracy runs from the Ministry of Defense at the top all the way down through local units within the military. There is a police bureaucracy which takes two forms—one a civilian police, or militia; the other a secret police, or KGB—both of which are centrally run from heavily staffed offices in Moscow, and by staff at all levels down to the local unit.

Finally, there is the Party apparatus, whose job is to supervise all this. The Party apparatus, by most estimates, has in the vicinity of 200,000 to 250,000 full-time officials coordinated by the Secretariat of the Central Committee in Moscow. Each level has its own bureaucracy, encompassing republic Party organizations, provincial Party organizations, city Party organizations, district organizations within cities, and Party organizations throughout the countryside. Only the smallest Party organizations are staffed by people who are not full-time officials; almost all others are staffed by full-time Party functionaries.

A fundamental distinction has to be made between being a Party member and being a Party official. There are many millions (the latest figures are somewhere around 19 or 20 million) of card-carrying members of the Communist Party of the Soviet Union. But there are only several hundred thousand full-time officials of the Party apparatus. Many of the officials whom they supervise within these various other bureaucracies are members of the Party, but their full-time job is not staffing the Communist Party apparatus itself.

Politics in the USSR is channeled through these institutions. The Soviet Union is what might be called an official political culture, in which the full-time officials are the ones who count politically. If there are individuals within the population who are disgruntled and want to make their needs known, they must channel them through this officialdom. Officialdom, in turn, will decide what happens to them.

In other words, the Martin Luther King phenomenon could not have occurred in the Soviet Union without provoking an immediate crackdown. It is probably fair to say that if there had been no television in the United States, it would have been very difficult for the Martin Luther King phenomenon to have spread even here. It was the publicity it received that allowed people all over the country to learn what was happening to people in distant places, to identify with them, and to be mobilized. It is that kind of publicity and dramatization of demands that is forbidden in the Soviet Union. That is why I call it an official political culture.

But even within officialdom there is a distinct hierarchy. Officials at the lower levels—for instance, district leaders in small towns—tend to have little power outside their immediate domains. They have a great deal of power within their jurisdiction, but little power vis-a-vis those above them. The higher up you go in the hierarchy, the greater the likelihood that you will have power at the national level.

This is the vertical view of the hierarchy. There is another, a horizontal way of looking at it. Generally speaking, Party officials at any given level tend to be more powerful than officials of other bureaucracies at the same level. There are, of course, exceptions to this rule; for example, if the economy of a town is dominated by a large factory, the Party official in the city might be listened to less than the factory manager, who says, "It can't be done—you've got to do it my way." But it is generally the rule in Soviet politics that the Party officials at a given level are going to be more powerful individuals within the political system as a whole than are other officials at the same level.

Struggles among officials at the same level are constant, not because the system is flying apart (I don't believe it is) but because that's the nature of politics. Politics is struggle over the allocation of scarce values, whatever those values may be, economic or otherwise. When you are trying to run a society with over a quarter of a billion people, over an expanse of land that covers one-sixth of the earth's land surface, there will naturally be differences of opinion, of priority, and of temperament—differences that are bound to fuel political struggles.

In struggles among officials at the same level, the tendency will be for those contending among themselves to appeal upward for political support. They will appeal to the higher levels in the political hierarchy within their bureaucracy and, if they can, also within the Party apparatus. For example, if the local Party official in a given city is squaring off against the manager of a large factory, the factory manager is going to appeal to his ministerial superiors in Moscow to try to get the Central Committee to rein in that local Party official or to make a decision favoring the manager over the *apparatchik*.

Similarly, the Party official will look upward within his hierarchy for support. He may not go all the way to the Central Committee; he may not need to. He may go to the provincial level or the republic level in an effort to get one of his superiors to intervene on his behalf at the expense of whomever he is battling with at the moment.

The possible bases for an appeal are manifold. It could be based upon economic or administrative rationality: "This is the most efficient way to spend our funds; this is the best way to organize the implementation of these decisions." It could be based upon claims regarding social justice: "The workers in our district are making less than the peasants; this shouldn't be—we are a workers' state, after all. We should give less of a wage increase to the peasants in the next Five

Year Plan and more to the workers." It could be based upon political wisdom, such as, "We are getting reports from our local police agencies that a lot of grumbling is being heard in the factories, and we think such and such a policy is wise—economic rationality be damned." It could be based upon institutional loyalties rather than social ideas, political caution, or economic efficiency. For example: "This guy is an egotistical manager who has been giving me a hard time for a long time and obviously does not realize the importance of Party control or Party supervision."

Or it could be based upon personal ties. The local Party official, for instance, could attempt to invoke support from whomever he considers to be his political patron. This is not a random phenomenon. Vertically organized networks of patron-client ties run through all of these bureaucracies; I would define them as one of the most fundamental features of Soviet political life. To understand Soviet politics by simply looking at an organization chart—though that is a beginning—is impossible, for competition within and between these bureaucracies is continuous. Those networks of clients attached to powerful individuals above them in the hierarchy may well, in any given case, cross bureaucratic lines of jurisdiction.

Gorbachev, to put it most simply, may have clients, i.e., those who are beholden to him for their jobs, in many bureaucracies. Certainly we know that Brezhnev had clients throughout the bureaucracies. Gorbachev will try to place his clients in the bureaucracies in order to do what is a fundamental, though certainly not the only, task of a higher ranking Party official in the Soviet Union—to build a political machine. Patronage allocation, the hiring and firing of personnel, and the patron-client ties that result are fundamental to the process of political machine building at the top. Indeed, top level politics within the Politburo and within the higher reaches of the Central Committee of the Party can be looked upon, for certain purposes, as a process of competitive machine building.

So far we have been looking from the bottom up. Now let us reverse directions and look from the top down. From the top down, the view of Soviet politics as machine politics is clearer. The leading decision-making bodies at the top of the system are the Politburo, which is comprised of the elite representatives of each of the major bureaucracies in the system; the Secretariat of the Central Committee, which is the major Party unit in charge of personnel control (among other things); the Defense Council, which is composed of an inner core of the Politburo with primary responsibility for defense issues; and the Presidium of the Council of Ministers.

The Council of Ministers is the chief overseeing body of the entire economic bureaucracy. The Presidium of the Council of Ministers brings together the most important planners and political overseers of this entire structure. They have considerable political weight, though they do not by any means outweigh the Politburo or Secretariat. Collectively these bodies bring together the top representatives of all the major bureaucracies. This, then, is the elite of the elite. Out of hundreds of thousands (if not more) of officials we are now focused on the few score officials, fifty to one hundred at the most—the top-level officials who constitute these four top-level bodies.

Over the past twenty years—the years of Brezhnevism—relations among these individuals and bureaucracies were generally more or less cooperative. This is not to say there was no conflict. There was. But, given the inevitability of conflict, the question is whether there is a relatively cooperative form of political interaction that keeps the conflict within bounds. Brezhnevism kept it in bounds.

Those cooperative relations were largely a product of his decision-making style, which was ultimately based on an unwillingness to rock the boat. And for this reason Brezhnev had less need to concentrate power or to engage in far-reaching political confrontations.

By Soviet standards, Brezhnev's was a relatively relaxed administration. A perspective on this can be gained by comparing the Brezhnev years with the Stalin or Khrushchev years. But Brezhnevism was an exception to all previous patterns, and it had its costs, among other things, in the legacies it left to its successors. In addition to the serious need for reforms in the economy during the Brezhnev era, there was the corruption of Soviet officialdom, though it existed in varying degrees. And a certain amount of demoralization among those seeking political mobility within these bureaucracies also took place.

To understand how this system might interact with whatever reforms Gorbachev might wish to undertake, one should think in terms of the imperatives of political machine building. For example, suppose Gorbachev wants to reform the economy and "get the country moving again." Everything we know supports the view that this is indeed the case. If so, Gorbachev will have to concentrate power. He will need to build a political machine that will allow him to pull rank, to purge or discipline the intransigents, to enforce his will, and to do something that is not often thought about or talked about in this context: to get his programs implemented throughout the huge, far-flung, very inefficient bureaucratic hierarchy.

He must bring in people who are not only beholden to him for their new jobs but who also share his general orientation, who agree with his view that what is needed now is to get the country moving again. He needs people who agree that the country cannot afford to continue a relaxed style of political administration. In many instances these will be individuals with whom Gorbachev has worked in the past and with whom he therefore shares experiences and old-boy ties, and, partly for that reason, shares a common orientation as well. In other instances, he may bring in people whom he knows, through reports of trusted associates, share his general outlook.

Political machine building is, of course, not unique to the Soviet Union. We first think of that term in its American context: the Tammany Hall politicians, the Richard Daleys, the Huey Longs, and so on. In fact, a comparative study of Chicago and Leningrad—Chicago under Daley and Leningrad under Romanov—would be fascinating and revealing (the two even looked alike!).

To be effective, a Soviet leader's political machine must transcend any one bureaucracy, but it must include the Party apparatus. When Andropov came to power, he had a long-established network of clients and supporters in the KGB and, within a restricted range of agencies, in the Party apparatus. But Andropov's power liability was that he had not had sufficiently diverse experience in the Party apparatus to have built up a large clientele among its members. Part of the reason, I think, that Andropov was moving so slowly on policy changes and surprised many people with the tepidness of the reform proposals that ultimately came out of his regime, was that he was moving forward to consolidate power and to build a political machine before getting into policy innovation.

Andropov was trying to build up for himself within the Party apparatus and within segments of the state bureaucracy a network of clients that would supplement the existing clientele network within the secret police. It is necessary to build up support in the Central Committee Secretariat, in key positions within the Council of Ministers, in the republic- and province-level Party organizations, and, if you're smart, in the military and police oversight organizations.

Power is quite diffused within the Soviet bureaucracy. Power is not simply the ability to get a committee to agree with your recommendations and to enact them. Many policies can be enacted but go absolutely nowhere if they are not implemented. Power, then, is the ability to get support at both stages—at the enactment stage and at the implementation stage. A leader will want to know that he can trust his clientele networks to see to the implementation of his policies by the various bureaucracies.

Though the Party apparatus supervises this huge economic bureaucracy, it is necessary to have clients not only in the Party apparatus but in the other bureaucracies as well. Not every position must be filled by a client, but there must be enough so that if there is a fundamental obstruction in the implementation of your policy at one of the critical bottleneck points, one of your clients will know about it and, rather than concealing it, will report it.

Why should this matter to a Soviet leader? After all, if he can simply consolidate his power and get enough clients in key positions near the top so that he cannot be toppled, why does he care about this task of building a political machine? Well, one reason might be simply idealism and self-image. That is, he might genuinely want to see the country better managed, to see it moving again (certainly Khrushchev did), and therefore might very much want to create the necessary political preconditions and work those sixteen to eighteen hours a day required to do a good job by his standards.

But there is more to it than just idealism. There is a further imperative that I will call authority building. We can distinguish between power and authority in the following sense: Power is the ability to pull rank; authority is the ability to persuade people that you are doing a good job, that you have the answers to the problems facing the regime, that you know enough not only about problem solving but also about political consensus building to grasp a problem intellectually and build a political coalition to support your approach to the problem.

Authority building then is very close to the notion of legitimacy. A leader not only has to be able to pull rank, he also has to be able to legitimize his leadership. In a terroristic regime you may not have to do that. If a police apparatus is using terror against officialdom, you need not worry about whether politicos think your policies are effective or not, whether they think that you're a good consensus builder or not. People are sufficiently off balance and terrorized; they would not dare to defy you.

Probably the most important distinction between post-Stalin politics and Stalinist politics is the end of terror as an instrument of policy. People are still thrown into labor camps for dissent, but no longer are millions of people thrown into labor camps for nothing. People are still fired from their jobs (and if you fire a lot of people at once, everyone in the West will call it a purge), but they're not shot in the back of the neck.

Politics in the Soviet Union were fundamentally transformed as a result of that change. One consequence was that the imperative for a leader to demonstrate his effectiveness as a problem solver and political coalition builder rose correspondingly. That is not to say that building legitimacy and authority as a leader is more important than consolidating power. I don't know of many ways that we could effectively measure the relative importance of the two; but the behavior of Soviet leaders since Stalin indicates that both are important.

The Politburo is not composed of lackeys. On the contrary, it includes the head of the Party and about a dozen other people, many of whom have independent power bases or established prestige, and who are themselves protecting their political positions by engaging in competitive political machine building. If the Party leader proves ineffective, or if he alienates too many of his associates, he may lose the support of those associates in the Politburo and of the political machines that they have built up. Khrushchev found this to be the case. In 1957 he brought Brezhnev into a leading position in national politics and over time built him up; yet Brezhnev was one of the leaders of the group that overthrew Khrushchev seven years later.

An interesting relationship between authority and power prevails in Soviet elite politics. If you have too little power, if you have not built a sufficiently far-flung political machine in the bureaucracies, your programs will not be faithfully carried out. And if your programs are undermined, your authority will be undermined as well, because you will be the one to be blamed if things go wrong, just as you are the one who demands the credit if things go well. Of course, you may try to shift the blame, but you will nevertheless be on the defensive.

This is the kind of situation Brezhnev faced in the mid-1970s. He responded by adroitly broadening his political base to a much more conservative but very powerful coalition. That change was in part responsible for the considerable drift in policy and the degeneration in the quality of the results of that policy over the last seven years of the Brezhnev regime.

Brezhnev used power to defend against declining authority. Gorbachev is using authority to build up his power. If you have a lot of authority—which I believe Gorbachev does, and he has a mandate to improve the situation—you can use that authority to build up your political machine by saying, "If I am to fulfill this mandate, I have got to have my people in key places to do it."

Let us turn then to an examination of the Gorbachev leadership, to the characteristics of his apparent coalition of supporters in the Politburo and Secretariat, and the implications of those characteristics for Gorbachev's ability to fulfill his mandate.

An outsider cannot be sure just which members of the Politburo and Secretariat can be counted as "Gorbachev men." But if we compare the top leadership with the individuals who ran the show six years ago, we find a number of new faces, any or all of whom may be part of the broad coalition supportive of Gorbachev's leadership and mandate. These new faces would include the following eleven men:

M. S. Gorbachev	General Secretary
E. K. Ligachev	Politburo member
E. A. Shevardnadze	Politburo member
G. P. Razumovsky	Politburo member
G. A. Aliev	Politburo member
V. I. Vorotnikov	Politburo member
B. N. El'tsin	Secretary of Central Committee
N. I. Ryzhkov	Politburo member
V. M. Chebrikov	Politburo member
L. N. Zaikov	Secretary of Central Committee
V. P. Nikonov	Secretary of Central Committee

What are some of the attributes of these eleven relative newcomers to the top leadership? One attribute is age. One of these men is 65 years old; one is 49 years old; the other nine are between 54 and 62 years of age. This group is on average 15 to 20 years younger than the Brezhnev generation, so that they are likely to run the show for at least the next decade.

A second feature of this group is the political generation to which they belong. For the most part, they began their political careers after

World War II or after Stalin's death. They are not products of the early Stalin era, when social transformation and terror were the main items on the policy agenda. Rather, they are products of an era dominated by the search for a stable, dynamic, efficient government, and the search for global power, economic prosperity, and peace. The main task of the post-Stalin era has been to synthesize these goals of peace, prosperity, and strength. Partly for this reason, these are men who have abundant experience working with specialists and with managers of advanced technological processes. They are consequently more self-confident than their elders about their ability to manage complexity.

Yet this is also a diverse group in terms of the skills they have exercised during their political careers. They are a blend of technocratic types and enforcers. Of the eleven men in this coalition, we can count six as Party officials with technical experiences, and five as Party officials with enforcer (or personnel manager) backgrounds.

Who are the technocrats? First, there is Gorbachev himself. Fifty-four years old in 1985, he holds degrees in both agronomy and law and has had some two decades of experience overseeing agricultural affairs in the province of Stavropol', one of the leading agricultural regions of the Russian Republic. Second, there is Comrade Vorotnikov, 59 years old. His training as an aircraft engineer was followed by two decades of experience in engineering, and then political, work in large factories. He spent four years as first deputy chairman of the Russian Republic Council of Ministers and is now chairman of that body. Third, there is Comrade Ryzhkov, 56 years old. He graduated from the Urals Polytechnical Institute and then spent 25 years working his way up in engineering and administrative positions within Uralmash, a huge machine-building complex in Sverdlovsk. He spent the years 1975 to 1979 working in the Ministry of Heavy Machine–Building, and 1979 to 1983 in the State Planning Committee, before being appointed head of the department of the Central Committee that oversees the economy.

A fourth member of this technically experienced subgroup is Comrade El'tsin. Fifty-four years old, he spent thirteen years in the construction industry in the Urals region before beginning a twenty-year Party career that led to his recent appointment as head of the Construction Department of the Central Committee. Fifth, there is Comrade Zaikov. A relatively old 62, he graduated from the Leningrad Engineering and Economics Institute and then spent 26 years working his way up in technical and managerial positions in Leningrad enterprises associated with the military-industrial complex. He then became mayor of Leningrad. Appointment as head of the Leningrad Party organization followed, and he is currently head of the Central Committee department that supervises the work of the military-industrial complex. Finally, there is Comrade Nikonov, 56 years old. He graduated from the Azov-Black Sea Agricultural Institute, after which he worked for ten years as an agronomist and agricultural administrator and then spent nineteen years in regional Party work. In 1979 he returned to functional administration at the highest levels as Deputy Minister of Agriculture of the USSR, then RSFSR Minister of Agriculture, and then Central Committee Secretary for Agriculture and the Agro-Industrial Complex.

These six people, then, have each had about a quarter century of experience working in both political and technical positions within various sectors of the economy in an era when the main imperative was to increase the level of sophistication of the technologies within those sectors. That they are experienced and comfortable with advanced technology is clear. It is important to bear in mind, however, that they are also Party professionals—Party organization men—and that means that for them Party leadership of the economy is a given. It is taken for granted; it is the way things are done in the Soviet Union.

Don't expect these people, whatever they may think of technological imperatives requiring greater decentralization of the economy, to reject Party leadership of the economy. They will be adjusting the way in which the Party plays this role; they won't reject Party control in principle or even in practice. The same is true of central planning. These are people whose entire lives have been spent in a centralized system—a system in which they believe. They have lost confidence in the current level of overcentralization of that planning, but the fact of central planning—and, by most comparative standards, a rather high level of central planning—is taken by them as desirable and necessary.

Another consequence of their being Party professionals is that they have political skills and political perspectives. They don't look at problem solving purely from the perspective of technological or economic rationality. In that respect, they are really quite different from capitalist branch managers who are looking primarily at the bottom line. These people have been trained to believe that you look first at the political and social implications of various solutions to economic problems. If those are tolerable, then you make the choice based on criteria of economic rationality.

Another fact to bear in mind is that these people are tough, tough hierarchs. They are not "children of the kibbutz." They are statists through and through. They will be no more tolerant of anti-system dissidents than were Brezhnev, Andropov, or Chernenko. In this respect there is no generation gap. They will be as willing as their predecessors to crush dissidents like bugs.

Indeed, I heard someone complain on the radio that Gorbachev was being likened to John F. Kennedy, and he considered it a thoroughly obnoxious parallel: "Gorbachev's not John Kennedy, he's J. R. Ewing." Well, when people make these analogies between Gorbachev and Kennedy, they typically say, "He is a *Soviet* John F. Kennedy." That is to say, in the Soviet context, according to Soviet political predispositions and preferences, he is viewed as someone who is likely to get the country moving again. In that respect he is a Soviet John Kennedy, but taken in an absolute sense—looking at the kinds of values he has had to internalize in order to rise within the system, and those values he has obviously embraced in order to rise within the system—it is important to bear in mind that he is going to be much closer to J. R. Ewing.

And yet, in spite of the fact that the new generation takes Party leadership and central planning for granted, believes in the primacy of politics in their basic approach to problem solving, and is tough, statist, and has a hierarchical orientation, these people are going to be more comfortable with advanced technology and complexity. They will also be more receptive to the advice of specialists who have long advocated trying different approaches to problem solving, who have advocated getting beyond the dogma and conventional wisdom of the past and experimenting with different ways of structuring the economy so that it will work better—even if that means depriving certain hierarchies of what in the past had been their inalienable rights.

Gorbachev's task, however, is not simply to come up with new ways of dealing with problems and to get people lined up behind them, but also to build a political machine. The other five people in this group of eleven are probably valued less for their technical competence than for their proven abilities as political enforcers and personnel managers. They are the kind of men who will help Gorbachev build such a machine.

Let us look at these other five. Ligachev, the elder statesman of the group, is 65 years old. He has spent 35 of the last 41 years in Party organization work in Tomsk and Novosibirsk, provinces in Siberia. Under Andropov he was brought to Moscow to take charge of cadres control (personnel control), and he has done a wonderful job of it from the standpoint of Gorbachev and Andropov. He was frequently sent out to the provinces to preside over meetings at which the heads of local Party organizations were fired and replaced. He has been, if you will, the hatchet man.

In recent months, Ligachev has been transferred to the position of chief ideologist of the regime. No longer as involved in day-to-day personnel control activities, he is now something of a watchdog—probably *the* watchdog—not over ideology but over the general personnel shifting process. Ligachev is not someone we think of when we talk of the new technologically oriented elite, but he is when we talk of the imperatives of political machine building.

We have seen a good deal of Eduard Shevardnadze, who is 57 years old. Until June of 1985 he had spent his entire career—39 years—in Georgian Republic Party and police work. He surprised all of us when he was suddenly appointed Foreign Minister, replacing Andrei Gromyko. There are several possible explanations for his appointment. One is that Gorbachev simply wanted Gromyko out of the way so that he could proceed to develop his own foreign policy. A more substantive explanation is that with his public relations skills and his Georgian background and relaxed manner, Shevardnadze can be extremely useful in promoting any alternative foreign policy that Gorbachev has in mind. The third explanation, and the one to which I am partial, is that Shevardnadze is the Ligachev of the Foreign Ministry. His lack of experience in foreign affairs was not viewed as a serious liability because no alternative foreign policy had yet been formulated in Moscow. Besides, Gorbachev, after his successful Canadian and British tours, had perhaps come to conclude that this was a piece of cake—that to make some real gains all you needed was a new style.

Shevardnadze had been a very skilled leader of a long anti-corruption drive in the Georgian Republic. It is not that the Foreign Ministry is corrupted in the way the Georgian Party organization had been, but rather that Shevardnadze had proven himself to be a very good personnel control man, very good at rejuvenating the cadres of an entire political organization—and that is probably one of his tasks in the Foreign Ministry. After all, Gromyko had been Foreign Minister since 1957 and had built his own machine within that ministry, so that changing the basic organizational biases of the institution requires more than just getting rid of the top man—it requires that dozens be replaced. I suspect that it is Shevardnadze's job to identify the dozens that need to be replaced and to help replace them.

Then there is Comrade Razumovsky, only 49 years old. He spent over two decades in leading Party and government positions in a major province in southern Russia. In 1983, when the leader of Krasnodar was fired and placed under house arrest on corruption charges, Razumovsky was sent there to purge and rejuvenate the Party and state apparatus, which had become one of the most corrupted Party organizations of the Russian Republic. Apparently he did quite well, because we are told that there are now a lot of new faces in the Krasnodar Party organization—again, a man valued not so much for his technological skills as for his role as political enforcer.

Next is Comrade Aliev, 62 years old in 1985. He spent 41 years in Party and KGB work in the Transcaucasian republic of Azerbaidzhan, another of the most corrupt areas of the USSR. He did an excellent job, not only regenerating momentum in the local economy but rejuvenating personnel within the Party organization, thereby gaining a reputation as a bright administrator and an active combatter of corruption. In 1982, only weeks after Brezhnev died, he was brought to Moscow to be First Deputy Chairman of the Council of Ministers—in effect, the vice-president of the economic bureaucracy—and promptly put in charge of the massive project of breaking the bottlenecks in the Soviet transportation system. Here then is a man valued for his skills both as an administrator and as a political enforcer.

Finally there is Comrade Chebrikov, 62 years old and head of the KGB. His earlier career was in Party organization, but he had spent the last sixteen years working his way to the top of the KGB—a man definitely valued as an enforcer, not as a technocrat. Bear in mind that just as the technocrats are *Party* technocrats, so the enforcers are Party men by training. They take for granted that the machine is Party led, not police led, that the police are an important instrument of the regime in enforcing what is defined as order and in transforming political organizations that are deemed to be out of control, but they do not define the issue as Party versus police. They define it rather as a coalition of Party officials and police officials created to advance common goals. That is a viewpoint that all eleven of these people share.

This group of eleven politicians is overwhelmingly provincial in background. Here are just a few examples: Gorbachev spent 23 of the last 30 years in a province of southern Russia; Ligachev, 35 of the last 41 years in Siberia. Shevardnadze spent all of the last 39 years in the provinces; Ryzhkov, 25 of the last 35; El'tsin, over 24 of the last 30; and Aliev, 41 of the last 44 years of his life.

This marks a change: Before the Brezhnev era, the most common personnel policy of the regime was to rotate Party officials back and forth between work in Moscow and work in the provinces, and also to post them sequentially to many different provinces. They were never to be limited exclusively to a central or a narrowly provincial perspective. They were never kept in one provincial party organization for a quarter of a century, as many of these people were. From 1955 to 1978, for example, Gorbachev worked nowhere but in Stavropol', in southern Russia.

Party officials back in the Khrushchev and Stalin eras would be used more as plenipotentiaries and sent from a Party organization in one part of the country to another in a different part of the country. They thus developed a varied perspective. This is the first leadership to be dominated by people whose experience has been overwhelmingly provincial—and narrowly provincial at that. They consequently may have a rather oversimplified view of national problems, but from the standpoint of policy innovation, that may be best.

In his book, *Development Projects Observed*, Albert Hirschman wrote that the best way to get policymakers to take bold initiatives is to make sure they are to a certain extent ignorant. If they have too much information about all the complexities involved, they are likely to be paralyzed with fear of risk-taking. You must therefore place in positions of authority people who do not have so strong a sense of ambiguity about things that they cannot make tough decisions. Maybe that is what is needed in the present Soviet context. One thing is sure: Coming from the provinces, the Gorbachev team has a vivid view of overcentralization. Stationed in the provinces and having to deal constantly with the ministries in Moscow, they acquired a real sense of frustration with the bureaucratization and overcentralization of the system.

These men have other advantages as a result of their provincial experience and bias. Because they were in the same posts for so long, they know the ins and outs of local Party organization. They know where the key bottlenecks are. They know what kinds of informal relationships can develop within a local political group. Ligachev, for instance, knows the Novosibirsk and Tomsk Party organizations intimately. In Gogol's *Inspector General*, the inspector general arrives from St. Petersburg, and everyone goes through an elaborate charade to deceive him. Well, no one can pull a similar stunt on Ligachev in Tomsk or Novosibirsk. He knows every skeleton in every closet.

These people, then, have the ability and the knowledge to be political enforcers. They also understand how far the corruption of local Party organizations has gone. That is a very important consideration. If you are ignorant of the extent of local or regional corruption you may underestimate the difficulty of getting an innovative policy faithfully implemented. These people know, and perhaps that is one of the reasons Gorbachev is moving so slowly on policy innovation but quickly on the building of a political machine.

There is still another striking attribute of this group as compared to the Brezhnev leadership. They have far fewer personal, "old-boy" ties with the military than did their predecessors. Some of them have extensive experience on the industrial side of the military-industrial complex. And all of them are products of a system in which core Party and military values of hierarchy, order, toughness, and discipline are shared.

In considering the changing of resource allocation or defense policy, it is important to recall that the Brezhnev generation, with Brezhnev himself as the perfect example, had ties from World War II—battle ties—for which simple political association cannot easily substitute. Those nostalgic personal ties with military commanders affected Brezhnev's political and policy choices. Because they do not for the most part have those kinds of ties, the Gorbachev team may well be much freer of commitments to the military sector and much less identified with the Brezhnev-era "deal" with the military.

Thus a pattern seems to be emerging: What we have is a coalition of Party technocrats and Party enforcers. This is ideal for Gorbachev's current purposes. He can simultaneously encourage new thinking about policy and concentrate power in a political machine of his own—a machine that will carry out his policies and augment his authority rather than undermining it.

This will not, of course, be easy. For one thing, the Gorbachev team is not united by shared experience. Rather, it is united largely by shared values based on their common reaction to the current situation, which might be stated as, "This economy has dragged for too long; it is not desirable for it to do so, nor is it necessary that it continue to do so. We can do better than this. Let's start doing it."

On the other hand, Brezhnev's ties with others in his leadership team were based on shared experience. In many cases these ties went back to his service in Kazakhstan, Moldavia, and the Ukraine. He brought people to Moscow to head Central Committee departments or to be Politburo members, or he found people still in the Politburo after Khrushchev with whom he shared common experiences. These were people on whom he could count, not only because they shared common reactions but, more importantly, because they had been working together for some thirty years.

The Gorbachev team, with just one or two exceptions, have not been working together at all except in the most recent years. One has been out in Siberia, another in Leningrad, several in the Urals, one in the Georgian Republic, another in Azerbaidzhan. Should the policies advanced by this coalition start to fail, this group might not have the kind of glue that held the Brezhnev group together, and political opportunism could rear its head.

At this point there is no denying that Gorbachev has tremendous authority and rapidly growing power. He presently has a mandate, but I would predict that his authority will dissipate if his policies fail to work. He will probably have a two- to three-year honeymoon period in which to start delivering on his innovative policies. If he fails to deliver, he may not lose his job, but he will be on the political defensive, with fewer old-boy political allies to draw on.

In sum, Soviet elite politics require that a Soviet leader engage simultaneously in political machine building and in political authority building. Gorbachev came to power with a mandate that gave him instant authority. He is now in a race against time to build the political machine required to sustain that authority.

SOVIET SOCIETY IN TRANSITION

El Lissitzky, *1922*

GAIL W. LAPIDUS

n the year 1981, an unusual article appeared in the Soviet Communist Party's major theoretical journal under the authorship of Politburo member, and subsequently General Secretary of the Party, Konstantin Chernenko. For possibly the first time since Lenin introduced NEP (New Economic Policy) in 1921 to quell domestic discontent, a key member of the Soviet political elite openly referred to the possibility of internal crisis in the USSR. If the Party failed to provide proper leadership, Chernenko warned in this article, it risked losing its mass support and could face "the danger of social tension and of political and socio-economic crisis."

Chernenko's concern reflected a widespread mood of malaise and anxiety evident within broad segments of the Soviet elite during the last years of Brezhnev's rule. Turmoil in Poland served as a sharp reminder that accumulating problems, if not successfully addressed, could provoke serious social instability.

Chernenko's comments also appeared to offer authoritative support for the apocalyptic images of the Soviet scene proffered by a number of Western commentators who affirmed that the Soviet Union in the late Brezhnev era was experiencing a profound systemic crisis. Western writings about the Soviet system have repeatedly used the term "crisis" to describe a wide variety of political and social problems, from economic slowdown to deteriorating health care, to nationality tensions. What was new was the suggestion that the structural, cumulative, and seemingly irreversible nature of these problems now made them unmanageable—that, in effect, the Soviet Union faced a "revolutionary situation" of historic dimensions. This assessment, in turn, has important implications for American policy toward the USSR. If the threat of instability and crisis was, as some argued, conducive to both internal reform and external moderation in Soviet behavior, American interests would be well served by policies which sought to exacerbate rather than alleviate Soviet problems.

The tendency to view Soviet problems in apocalyptic terms has been so recurrent a feature of American perceptions of the Soviet scene that we have tended to neglect the very considerable sources of stability of the Soviet system. At the same time, stability should not be confused with rigidity, or lead us to ignore the very genuine pressures for change within the system. In this essay I will focus on the very real social problems with which Chernenko and his successors have been preoccupied and which have become a major focus of Gorbachev's early policy initiatives. I will propose that although the Soviet system confronts a set of major problems at this particular stage of its development—problems as severe and complex as those existing at any point since the death of Stalin in 1953—the danger of destabilization is extremely remote. Indeed, the new Gorbachev leadership has moved very quickly to address these problems, with a sense of urgency and a number of fresh initiatives that constitute a real departure from previous behavior.

The Soviet Union in the Gorbachev era is a country in the midst of a major transition, a transition whose scope and outcome remain uncertain, but one which extends from the composition of its political elite to key economic institutions and policies and to the social values and social policies that have contributed so critically to the stability of the Soviet system. Indeed, to fully appreciate the potential impact of Gorbachev's political agenda it is helpful to view it in the broader context of Soviet development in the post-Stalin period.

For the Soviet political elite, as for the Soviet population generally, the post-Stalin years, until the late 1970s, were in many respects a golden era in Soviet history. By the time of Stalin's death a number of fundamental crises had been successfully surmounted, from the traumas of collectivization, of the purges, and of

World War II, to the trauma of Stalin's own departure from the political scene in 1953. Under Khrushchev and Brezhnev the Soviet Union entered a new stage of its development. It enjoyed a period of growing internal prosperity, a high degree of social and political stability after an epoch of turmoil and insecurity, and a more benign international environment in which it occupied an increasingly secure and powerful place.

Within the Soviet Union itself, the relaxation of terror diminished what had been a major source of alienation from the regime. A combination of rapid economic growth and expanding educational and occupational opportunities strengthened popular support for the Soviet system and made it possible to supplant to some extent the Stalinist reliance on coercion with a more secure and stable social base. Rapid rates of economic growth made it easier for the Soviet political leadership to allocate resources among competing priorities—investment, military power, and consumption—and among rival claimants, whether institutional bureaucracies, geographical and ethnic regions, or social classes. Not only could the leadership meet the population's modest expectations for improved living standards; it could also insure security of employment (and the absence of unemployment), low and stable prices for basic commodities—from food, to rent, to social services—and a high level of public order.

Moreover, by significantly enhancing the power and status of the Soviet Union in the international arena, the Soviet leadership could also tap strong sentiments of patriotism and pride within the population as a whole. It was therefore in a position to deal rather easily with what could have been significant challenges to its political rule, including an unprecedented level of intelligentsia dissent. Although the dissident movement reached its apex during the period of detente, it was disposed of harshly but—from the point of view of the leadership—rather successfully.

By the late Brezhnev period, however, this entire picture had changed dramatically. The Soviet leadership confronted an increasingly bleak prospect on both the domestic and the international scene. Four factors played a key role in this transformation.

First and foremost was the growing retardation of the Soviet economy, a retardation which had both a quantitative and a qualitative dimension. Slowing rates of economic growth forced hard choices among military expenditures, investment, and consumption, and adversely affected the ability of the Soviet leadership to provide the steady improvement in living standards that the Soviet population had come to expect. The growth of military spending slowed sharply in the late 1970s, provoking visible strain in Party-military relations, while the economy was increasingly deprived of the new investment needed to rejuvenate decaying industrial enterprises. Consumer dissatisfaction became especially pronounced and focused on the poor quality as well as the inadequate quantity of desired goods and services. As rising incomes and expectations created a demand for high quality goods and services that far exceeded the supply, a thriving "second economy" expanded to bridge the gap. At the same time, the food supply—a key element in the population's assessment of regime performance, and therefore an exceedingly delicate political as well as economic issue—was hard hit in the late 1970s and early 1980s by a series of poor harvests. Shortages of meat and dairy products produced widespread discontent and helped trigger a number of strikes and demonstrations, forcing the government to ration selected food products.

Technological backwardness compounded the problems of economic slowdown. Revolutionary developments in communications and other new technologies—such as the computer revolution—left the Soviet Union even further behind. Not only did Japan overtake the USSR in key measures of national income, but the economic dynamism of other Asian countries—from the People's Republic of China to South Korea to Taiwan to Malaysia—dramatized the shortcomings and indeed irrelevance of the once heralded Soviet economic model.

The pressures of external competition were accentuated even further by the deterioration of Soviet-American relations. The collapse of detente and the American military build-up launched under Carter and Reagan rekindled the fear that the United States would once again outstrip the USSR not only militarily but also in new technologies with significant future military potential.

A final source of malaise was the apparent incapacity of the Soviet leadership itself to address these problems adequately. An aging and frequently ailing political elite continued to hold tightly to the reins of power, frustrating the ambitions of a younger and more impatient political generation, while failing to come to grips with what were widely perceived as urgent needs. To make matters worse, corruption and scandal seemed to have penetrated to the very highest levels of the Soviet elite and touched the Politburo itself; only the KGB (Secret

Police) and the military appeared untarnished by revelations of abuse of official position.

Taken together, these trends had a corrosive impact on civic morale. The optimism of the Khrushchev era turned to pessimism about the Soviet future, disillusionment with official values, and a mood of cynicism, apathy, and malaise. Khrushchev's boast that by 1980 the Soviet population would enjoy the highest standard of living in the world now seemed hollow mockery, as Chernenko cautioned the drafters of the Party program to eliminate overly confident forecasts as well as excessive use of figures and minor details. While capitalism is doomed by history, he reminded his audience that it still had substantial reserves for development.

Low worker productivity and a high degree of apathy also reflect this mood of social malaise. In a highly publicized dialogue with factory workers Andropov warned that wage increases could not outstrip productivity. But the absence of effective material incentives erodes the motivation of workers to raise output. Moreover, severe shortcomings in the supply of goods and services divert a large share of the population's time and energy from production to procurement. While the growth of the "second economy" serves as a safety valve in reducing frustration, it also produces an unofficial and uncontrollable redistribution of resources and incomes that distorts central priorities.

The decline in civic morale had three elements. The first was the loss of optimism, the conviction that the system cannot live up to expectations, although there is little conviction that the United States or other capitalist systems offer a viable alternative. The second element was the loss of a sense of purpose—a result of the declining relevance and vitality of official ideology. Recent years have witnessed a widespread quest for alternative sources of values. Heightened interest in religion—evident in church attendance, in the growing use of religious symbolism, and the affirmation of moral and spiritual values—is one manifestation of this trend. It is also expressed in the renewed interest in national traditions and a general nostalgia for the past, dramatically illustrated by the rapid rise and massive membership of the grass-roots Society for the Preservation of Historical and Cultural Monuments. And it takes the form of other kinds of escapism, whether to personal relations, to parapsychology, to science fiction, or even to alcohol. The third element of the decline of civic morale is the erosion of social controls and individual self-discipline, evident in the whole gamut of social pathologies, from alcoholism to corruption, to violations of labor discipline, to theft of state property—in short, to the failure to internalize new social norms.

If the system of values that had earlier served as a source of social cohesion no longer served its original function, there were now real constraints on the ability of the leadership to resort to other means of social control. The use of coercion and mass terror on a large scale had been repudiated after Stalin's death. While the KGB remained a potent instrument for dealing with anything that could be construed as anti-regime activity, large areas of individual behavior increasingly fell within the domain of individual choice and outside the orbit of direct regime control.

The labor market offers one dramatic illustration of this trend. Massive movements of population to the southern regions of the country in search of better living conditions and higher incomes flew in the face of central economic priorities, which sought to move scarce labor to Siberia to help develop energy and other natural resources there. Yet another area of social behavior that had become important to the regime, family policy, proved equally resistant to central priorities. During a period in which the Soviet Union was experiencing a declining rate of population growth, particularly among the Russian and Baltic populations, rapid population growth was occurring instead among the largely Moslem populations of labor surplus in Central Asia, and there proved to be no easy way to reverse these trends. In these instances, as in a whole range of areas, the regime lacked the levers to enforce its priorities. Ideological exhortation proved inadequate to mobilize desired behavior; coercion was unavailable or inappropriate to the task; and the reliance on material incentives was sharply constrained by the economic slowdown. Neither higher wages nor enhanced social mobility could be held out as motivations for officially desired behavior.

Thus, the late Brezhnev period was marked by an accumulation of social and economic problems on the one hand, combined with the erosion of traditional instruments for dealing with them, on the other. These difficulties were further compounded by the absence of forceful and imaginative leadership that could break through the considerable bureaucratic inertia that constituted a formidable barrier to real change and elicit the mass enthusiasm and dedication that might halt the erosion of civic morale. In this respect, the Gorbachev succession constitutes a necessary, but not sufficient, condition for change.

Before turning to Gorbachev's strategy for addressing these problems, a few observations deserve to be restated. First, it is not the severity of any of these problems individually that constitutes a critical issue. At a number of points in its history the Soviet Union faced difficulties that were far more threatening to its security and survival: Collectivization could have produced the collapse of the Soviet system, and World War II could also have brought its demise. In comparison with these genuine crises, or comparable ones faced by other societies at other points in their histories, current Soviet difficulties are considerable less acute. To the extent that the term crisis is meaningful, it is a crisis of effectiveness rather than of survival.

Moreover, many of these problems are as much a product of Soviet successes as of Soviet failures, reflecting the presence of a new set of requirements associated with a new stage of development. They reflect the exhaustion of institutions and strategies that served well at earlier stages of development but have become a brake on current progress, which requires new forms of economic and social organization. Finally, these problems are also a product of the enormous aspirations of the Soviet system, both domestically and internationally. If the Soviet Union were content to remain a second-rate power, they would not prove nearly so acute. But it is the fact that the Soviet Union seeks to be a major global actor, indeed a superpower, and that it has also stimulated aspirations among its own people to enjoy living standards comparable to those of other advanced industrial societies that puts the system under extreme pressure to improve its performance. It is therefore the gap between current capabilities and ambitions that contributes to the pressures for change.

Gorbachev has brought a new sense of urgency as well as energy to addressing the problems outlined here. He is the beneficiary of unusual opportunities to alter the composition of the political elite, and the beneficiary as well of a widespread yearning for strong and decisive leadership to get the country moving again. Soviet political culture has long attached great value to strong, paternalistic, even authoritarian leadership. From the postwar generation of Soviet refugees to the current wave of emigrés, even among those most critical of the Soviet system, one encounters a pervasive unease with the individualistic, competitive, laissez-faire strains of American political culture and a tendency to view it as dangerously pluralistic and anarchic. For the Soviet population to have faced the death of three leaders in relatively rapid succession left a gnawing sense of anxiety and insecurity which Gorbachev has moved very quickly to eradicate. The accession of a comparatively young and energetic leader under these circumstances fills an important psychological as well as polit- ical void; the widespread desire for effectiveness constitutes one of his major political assets.

First and foremost on Gorbachev's political agenda is the need to radically improve the performance of the Soviet economy. This effort requires a combination of structural and policy changes which will increase both the incentives for successful performance and the pen- alties for failure. Such changes are likely to entail a further diminution of economic and social equality. For enterprise management it requires greater autonomy and greater accountability, and a restructuring of the larger economic bureaucracy. But serious economic reforms would have their most dramatic impact on the Soviet working class, not only by increasing wage differentials but by making job security depend- ent on work performance. A move in this direction would challenge a long-standing set of expectations that constitute at one and the same time a tremendous drag on economic efficiency and a major contri- bution to social stability. They are necessary to a revitalization of the economy, but they strike at one of the most basic guarantees of the Soviet system. While the scarcity of labor makes the specter of actual unemployment an unlikely one, serious economic reforms have a certain potential for social destabilization.

Similarly, measures to allow greater scope for private initiative in agriculture and the service sector also challenge deeply rooted values, which hold private economic activity to be virtually antisocial. Soviet publications are filled with lively controversy over whether it subverts the socialist economy and the values associated with it. This ongoing debate has been given added intensity by current efforts at economic reform in the People's Republic of China, which are followed with considerable but critical interest in the Soviet press.

But the initiatives on which I should like to focus attention are precisely those that seek to address the problems of social malaise. Gorbachev's speeches have insisted on the urgency of the issues, virtually accusing Brezhnev and Chernenko of in-

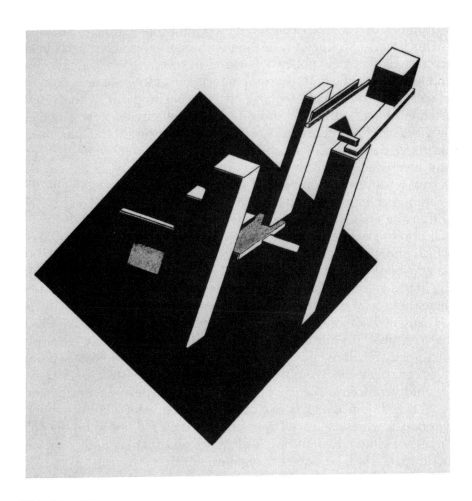

El Lissitzky, *1922*

ertia and ineffective half-measures in addressing internal difficulties. The first requisite of successfully attacking such problems, Gorbachev appears to be arguing, is to face them openly—through more frank discussions in the media, closer contact between the leadership and the population, and more effective use of public opinion surveys to ascertain popular attitudes and expectations. As is suggested by the unusually extensive Soviet media coverage of Gorbachev's press conference in Paris or of President Reagan's interview with Soviet reporters, Gorbachev's strategy is one of preemption as well; the suppresssion of information and the failure to address problems openly has not only contributed to domestic alienation but has created opportunities that can be exploited by foreign propaganda.

This broader strategy for dealing with internal problems has been accompanied by new policy departures in several specific areas. First and foremost is the massive campaign against alcoholism. A number of measures to combat excessive alcohol consumption, with its devastating impact on health and on labor productivity, were intitiated by Gorbachev's predecessors, but these were timid and piecemeal efforts by comparison with the scope and comprehensiveness of current measures. This campaign is intended not only to reduce the overall level of consumption of strong spirits, but to challenge the ubiquitous reliance on vodka to smooth business dealings, especially within the state, Party, and diplomatic elites. More fundamentally still, it represents an effort to alter the permissive climate of values, which offers social support to heavy drinking. The objective may not be wholly dissimilar to that achieved by the campaign against smoking in this country in recent years: a modest shift in values that offers increased social support to non-smokers in public settings.

Combined with the campaign against alcoholism is a massive attack on corruption. While this assault has its political utility during a succession in helping eliminate potential opponents and competitors, it is primarily intended as a signal that the period of drift, of anarchy, and of tolerance for the use of public office for personal enrichment is at an end. Joined as it is to a campaign for greater labor discipline, it serves to reassure Soviet workers that they are not to be the sole targets of a more demanding leadership, and that similarly exacting performance will be expected of elites.

A final but also significant element of Gorbachev's strategy for dealing with social malaise is the effort to bring expectations into closer line with real possibilities. The new Party program is one example of this effort: By placing the achievement of socialism, as well as of full communism, into a very distant future, and eliminating the more ambitious and utopian features of Khrushchev's 1961 program, the leadership is seeking to focus on a more limited and feasible set of objectives. Similarly, the new educational reforms, in which Gorbachev played a key role, seek to scale down excessive popular aspirations for upward social mobility. By shifting the focus of secondary training from academic to vocational pursuits, and making it clear that the performance of good blue-collar work is a worthy objective in life, the reforms are intended to reduce the widespread sense of frustration and alienation among young people whose aspirations for higher education and satisfying professional careers cannot be satisfied.

It remains unclear how the Gorbachev leadership will motivate the Soviet population to achieve the goals of rapid scientific and technical progress and increased labor productivity. While the new Five-Year Plan promises significant increases in consumer goods and services, it remains to be seen whether the combination of authoritarianism, pragmatism, and energetic leadership will suffice in addressing the problems of civic morale bequeathed by Gorbachev's predecessors.

PROBLEMS FACING THE SOVIET ECONOMY

A Kokorekin, "Komsomol Members Fight for Bolshevist Reconstruction of Transport!" *1931*

M A R I E   L A V I G N E

Mikhail Gorbachev is attempting to prepare the Soviet Union for the technological demands of the twenty-first century. If he is indeed to do so, many things will have to change. The first one to share this conviction is Gorbachev himself, as he has repeatedly stated since his accession to power.

Four general issues have to be addressed in order to estimate his chances of success:

In what shape does Gorbachev find the Soviet economy? Is it possible to reverse the continuing trend toward a slowdown of growth rates that was observable at the beginning of the seventies?

Can he effect radical (or even just substantial) economic reform? Since the first attempt by Leonid Brezhnev in 1965 all have failed; routine, inefficiency, red tape, numerous vested interests, have killed all efforts toward an improvement in management and planning. Beyond question, Gorbachev wants a fresh start. But can he succeed?

What is to happen to the Soviet citizen? Since Stalinist times he (and even more she!) has lived a hard life in a world of shortages and low consumption standards. Is the new leader to bring about better housing, fewer queues, more choice of goods and a greater variety of stores, and even—if wild expectations are to become real—a car in every family?

The fourth and last question is related to the outer world: Is the Soviet Union to be more deeply involved in world trade? And if so, how? The common view is that trade is indeed important to the Soviet Union—especially trade with the West, which supplies the Soviet Union with technology and food in exchange for oil, gas, and other raw materials. Does the Soviet Union have the export capacity to take this path? Does it make sense for the Western world to try to influence this scheme by restraining access to technologies (especially those having a strong impact on growth or export capacities) and/or by embargoing grain exports? Does the Soviet Union mean to modify the present distribution of its trade among its Western, Eastern, and Southern partners?

The answer to the question, "How is the Soviet economy doing in 1985?" is simple: Not well. As Gorbachev himself said at a conference on the economy last June, "One cannot help seeing that since the early 1970s certain difficulties began to be felt in economic development." According to CIA (Central Intelligence Agency) estimates, the annual growth of the Soviet Gross National Product (GNP) dropped from nearly 4 percent in the early seventies to less than 3 percent at the end of the seventies and has dropped to about 2 percent in the eighties. The Soviet figures are higher but show the same downward trend. What are the causes of this stagnation in the Soviet economy?

The Soviets refer to their failure to achieve "intensive growth" after decades of "extensive growth" in which heavy reliance was placed upon forced industrialization, massive investment, and extreme labor intensiveness. The extensive growth pattern is a legacy of the Stalinist system. In the thirties, when the Soviet Union had large untapped reserves of natural resources and a huge peasant population that could be put to work by compulsion in heavy industry—and when the levels of consumption could be kept at a minimum—it was possible to devote the largest possible share of the national income to investment growth.

The Soviet economy has never really shifted to a pattern whereby the increases in production would be achieved primarily through growth in overall productivity of labor and capital. The lack of productivity is also rooted in the general inefficiency of the system and a built-in reluctance of the workers to strive for greater output. (We will return to both these factors.) But before turning to the issue of reform, it is important to ask, Can the Soviets simply go on as they have in the past?

The traditional pattern is very wasteful. True, the Soviet Union is arguably the last frontier in the developed world with immense reserves of all types of strategic commodities: fuels, minerals, wood. The main weakness, however, lies in the location of these resources. They are primarily in Siberia, which compels the Soviet leaders to invest heavily in their development and extraction.

The Soviet Union also has a diversified industry, though it is technologically well below world standards, particularly in non-military goods. This industry is extremely energy-intensive and raw materials-intensive; it consumes, on average, about 30 to 40 percent more in fuels and materials than comparable Western industries. Finally, the Soviet Union has a large labor force, which, again on average, compares favorably with Western labor in terms of education and skill level.

The traditional path of Soviet growth has been to rely upon consumption of abundant materials rather than upon conservation of resources. Until recently there were no severe constraints that demanded the adoption of another strategy. In addition, the Soviet Union (unlike all Western industrialized countries) was not compelled to adjust as a consequence of the 1973–74 energy crisis. On the contrary, at least until the early eighties, the Soviet Union enjoyed high windfall gains from the crisis and its consequences. The USSR could sell oil at increased prices and thus benefit from the new prosperity of the Middle East oil exporters who happen to be its best customers for arms. Moreover, the Soviet Union benefited from increases in the price of gold. The absence of a need for drastic adjustment probably hampered reform attempts and suppressed consciousness of the existence of growing bottlenecks. These bottlenecks are now surfacing. Let us examine them more closely.

In the 1970–1980 period, available manpower increased by 24 million people. In the 1980s, the increase will be only 6 million—all of them in non-European parts of the USSR. Some schemes are now devised to involve pensioners in part-time work and to mobilize more women. But almost all women of working age are already at work, which has affected natality rates, as it is extremely difficult to combine professional work and child-rearing in the Soviet Union. It is now therefore vital to increase the *productivity* of all workers, not only so that growth rates can be maintained for the existing industries, but so that additional manpower can be allocated to underdeveloped sectors of the economy.

The share of investment in the national income (the Soviet aggregate for GNP) is already very high—over 25 percent—and cannot be increased. The official policy is to provide for a growth in consumption and to follow a cautious investment plan. There are four aspects to this policy.

First, huge investment projects are not to be undertaken. The volume of new investments is to be reduced, and reconstruction and revamping of enterprises are to take its place. This "modernization" is to amount to about 50 percent of total investment; it is currently one-third. Energy nevertheless remains a priority; consequently, costly projects in this field, such as the construction of new nuclear power stations, installation of additional gas pipelines, and drilling of offshore oil wells, are to be pursued. Even if energy-saving measures are implemented, the Soviet Union must still increase its production so that domestic and export requirements can be met.

Second, efforts are to be made to reduce "unfinished investments." These have traditionally been the plague of the Soviet investment policy. Projects are launched because the enterprises and their ministries have succeeded in having them written into the plan, but in fact they do not have the capacity (building materials, machinery, etc.) to realize them. Unfinished investments skyrocketed to 80 percent of total investment in the early eighties, and Gorbachev has made the decrease of this figure a high priority.

Third, the agricultural program launched in 1982, a legacy of Brezhnev, is still in force and should absorb over 30 percent of total investment. It comprises the supplying of agriculture with machinery, fertilizers, storage facilities, transport equipment, and land improvement measures. Here again, as in the energy sector, a mere reduction in waste could help, even if there were no increase in production. The waste of crops is indeed due to the lack of adequate equipment, but there are other causes, such as the peasants' general lack of interest in working collective farms.

And finally, as part of the program for improvement of living standards, investments are required for the services sector, and also in housing. Gorbachev has undertaken specific commitments on behalf of these goals.

The military sector currently consumes 12 to 16 percent of domestic GNP (taking the lower and the higher figure among Western estimates). Two points must be emphasized. First, there has been an acceleration in the growth of military expenditures over the past two years, and the budgetary discussion in the Soviet parliament (the Supreme Soviet) has stressed that fact. Second, an increase in military expenditures never benefits the civilian sector. In the West, firms working for the military sector are eager to derive profits from their achievements in this field by extending their expertise to the civilian sector. This spin-off does not occur in the Soviet Union. The only spillover is caused by the fact that some industries working for the defense sector are allowed to manufacture industrial consumption goods (for example, refrigerators and other household appliances) and to sell them through the trade outlets. Soviet citizens are well aware of this. They expect higher quality in those goods and try to get hold of them as soon as they appear in the general stores.

All of this explains why Gorbachev has said—in a much publicized trip to Leningrad, where he spoke with the workers—that just to keep even on living standards and to ensure the military requirements, the country would need a growth rate of 4 percent a year instead of the 3 percent that it is presently achieving with great difficulty. In order to do this, the Soviet economy has to be modernized. For this, a radical reform—or more precisely, as it is called now, a "restructuring"—is needed.

There have already been three rounds of reform; they are now in the middle of the third, launched under Andropov. Let us recall the basic features of the first, the 1965 version. In principle, those enterprises that actually produce the goods were to get more freedom, fewer compulsory planning indicators, and the right to retain a higher share of their profits. In turn, they were supposed to make good use of this freedom to implement the plan efficiently and to spontaneously propose "taut" plans, plans for a rational utilization of all their capacities. In fact, this scheme never worked. The planning indicators remained numerous and actually precluded autonomy for the enterprises. As a result, performance did not improve, and the traditional behavior of the enterprises remained unchanged. By deliberately concealing their real capacities and asking for more material resources than they really needed they went on trying to get the easiest possible plan to implement.

Underlying the reform pattern, there is the ever-unachieved dream: to reconcile the general interest (as expressed by the official authorities) with the interests of the enterprise and of the individuals. At all stages, it is believed that everybody should be willing to work for the perfect implementation of the perfect plan. But like most dreams, this one has not come true. There are many reasons for this.

Obviously, no perfect plan can be devised. The difficulties of planning are increasing over time. Stalinist Soviet Russia was an underdeveloped country, with huge potential resources and one dominant priority: to build the basic elements of a heavy industry in the shortest time. Now the economy is more complex. Still, the planners want to control most of the production. Over a million items are planned; 20 to 50 million are *priced*! To control this complex structure perfectly is impossible.

In the age of electronics, why should computers not provide a solution? In the Soviet Union itself, some experts advocate a wide introduction of mathematical methods into planning. But even apart from the fact that the computer technologies are lagging behind Western standards, and that the production of both hardware and software is insufficient, general computerized planning is not a way out. Even with the most sophisticated programs, the number of processes to be controlled is unmanageable—unless, of course, the conception of central planning changes. In addition, the *quality* of the data used by the Gosplan (State Planning Commission) is highly questionable because these data are provided by enterprises which, as we have learned, have every reason to conceal their capacity. The enterprises will never play against themselves: They will underestimate their real production potential by concealing the existence of machinery or material reserves so that they can fulfill the plan more easily; and conversely, they will, whenever possible, inflate their real performance so that they can receive bonuses.

Another reason can be identified at the enterprise level. We have just stated that the interests of the enterprises do not coincide with those of the society as expressed by the planning office. More generally, the enterprises are not interested in better quality; at present, everything they manufacture is sold, whatever its quality, because all production is allocated to users or consumers as specified in the plan. Should they, in spite of these disincentives, strive for better results, they are faced with many obstacles when they attempt to use their profits. For instance, they might wish to buy new equipment—selffinancing of small investments is expressly advocated as one potential utilization of profits—but they will not be able to find a supplier, because all production has already been allocated. The same applies to "social" investments such as the building of workers' dwellings, child-care houses for the children of the factorys' employees, etc.

The worst case of the contradiction between the interests of society and those of the enterprise is in the matter of innovation. The official theme is always the importance of technological progress—implementation of the results of science for use in production—but Soviet enterprises are not only reluctant to innovate, they have incentives to refrain from doing so. The costs of innovation are not taken into account in fixing prices. The usual way of measuring the output of an enterprise, an evaluation in "physical" units such as tons, is still widely applied although it was supposed to have been abolished in 1965. This is obviously a system that does not encourage technological progress. Many innovations, for example, are "weight-saving," such as substituting plastic for metal. Firms are induced to stick to routine and obsolete production processes in order to achieve performance indicators more easily.

Then there is the individual worker. What is true for the enterprise is also valid for the individual. The worker, like the enterprise, wants to fulfill his plan in the easiest way. Differentials in earnings tied to individual performance are slight. Moreover, the worker often prefers to spare his efforts so that he can engage in the "second economy" (all forms of moonlighting) after work or even during it. He is by no means afraid of losing his job as the probability of being fired is low. Should he be fired, jobs are easily available in an economy experiencing acute "manpower shortages" as well as the employment of excess manpower in the enterprises. ("Excess" is measured here in comparison with Western standards.)

In addressing these problems, Gorbachev immediately took the line of the 1984 Andropov "experiment" (as it was called in Russian). This program was itself a continuation of "improvements" initiated in 1979. Without detailing these very complicated schemes, let us note the three major ideas underlying the present experiment, which, according to a decree of June 12, 1985, is to be applicable to more than half of industry in 1986 (most of the consumer goods and services industries, and most of the machine-building sector). It is to be extended to all industry in 1987.

The first element of this plan relates to the importance of technological progress. The 1985 decree combines centralization (the plan

must provide for the production of modern goods and allocate the required resources for that at least six months before the beginning of the planned year) and price incentives to cover the increased costs of new, improved products. This would already represent a shift from the previous policy. The human factor is not forgotten. Gorbachev has called for a greater role in society for the engineer—for more prestige and for higher pay. At present there is little difference between the pay of an average worker and that of an engineer. In order to encourage enterprises, production of goods that meet the world standard (as evaluated by special "quality" committees) will be rewarded by high bonuses. Conversely, poor quality is to be punished by cuts in prices and reduction in bonus funds.

The second element, already outlined in the 1979 "mini reform," is to strengthen "contract discipline." The enterprises will be heavily fined if there are delays or if they do not deliver specified items according to standards agreed upon with the customer.

Finally, several measures attempt to restore the link between achievement and reward, both at the enterprise level and for the workers. The allocation of material resources for self-financed investments as well as for social projects realized by the enterprises is to be decentralized. The "brigade system" is to be intensified. In this system, which already encompasses about one-half of the industrial work force, small groups of workers or "brigades" organize their activities on the basis of "self-management" and are entitled to distribute the wage bill allotted to the brigade in accordance with the contribution of each member. The brigade system has, up to the present, had mixed results. In some cases productivity and individual wages have substantially increased. But in too many cases self-management has been hampered by shortages of raw materials, irregular supplies, and poor operation of the equipment.

There is little in this that is really new. Gorbachev has yet to convince the workers and enterprises that his modernization attempts will not be rendered sterile by the routine of the system. It seems that Gorbachev wants, for instance, to reduce the number of ministries and civil servants in the economic administration. He has already dismissed some ministers but without eliminating the ministries themselves. But so have his predecessors; can he go further and attack vested interests on a higher scale? After all, the powerful Soviet bureaucracy has much to lose in a radical reform, and even Gorbachev cannot cut into that empire without the support of new groups to counteract the resistance of the traditionalists. In addition, if he embarks on really radical reform, the immediate results are likely to be negative. The disorganization that will inevitably follow substantial changes will probably lower the rates of growth, create bottlenecks, and convey a sense of failure. The General Secretary is really on the razor's edge. At the moment his tactic seems to be to address the Soviet people, bypassing the Party and government officials. Will the Soviet citizen respond?

The condition of the Soviet people (and this also applies to the citizens of most of the other Eastern European countries) is characterized by numerous paradoxes. As they have been jokingly summarized by one Eastern European scholar:

- everybody is employed but nobody works;
- nobody works but the plan is fulfilled;
- the plan is fulfilled but there is nothing to be found in the shops;
- shops are empty but in every house you can find lots of goods;
- houses are full but people complain;
- people complain but the Party candidate gets 99.9 per cent of the vote.

Let us elaborate on some of these "paradoxes" before trying to evaluate the prospects for a change.

The first and essential point is that the Soviet citizen of working age, man or woman, is indeed employed, though not necessarily efficiently employed. Although the authorities wish to reduce the number of employees in the existing enterprises and to create new jobs in underdeveloped sectors (such as services), the enterprises are reluctant to decrease their staff for many reasons. The cost of manpower is not very high. The bad quality of supplies compels enterprises to maintain a great number of workers engaged in "auxiliary" jobs, such as repairs or adjusting inadequate materials to the needs of production by the manufacturing of spare parts. Deliveries are often irregular, so there are periods of low activity in the enterprise, followed by feverish work for the completion of the plan by the fixed date. Finally, most of the industrial enterprises are to "lend" a part of their workers to agriculture during the crop period, and this is another source of disorganization.

The Soviet workers know that they will always be able to get jobs. They change jobs very frequently; the rate of turnover is high, and the basic reason for this is not the lure of higher wages, but of better social benefits. Social benefits such as the availability of workers' dwellings, child-care facilities, summer vacation houses, etc., vary widely from one enterprise to another.

The Soviet citizen is thus literally incapable of understanding what unemployment may mean. Job security is taken for granted. Conversely, he or she cannot imagine what capitalist unemployment may mean and is therefore deeply convinced that if people do not work in Western countries, it must be by choice or laziness. This misconception is the source of bitter disappointment for many Soviet emigrés, who discover that it can be difficult to find a job in the West.

The downside of full employment and low efficiency of labor is, obviously, low salaries. It is very difficult to put this in Western terms because the rate of exchange between the ruble and the Western currencies is artificial, and also because the relative prices of goods in the West and in the Soviet Union are very different. The average salary in the industrial sector is about 200 rubles per month, or about $220 at the present rate of exchange. This seems terribly low, but one has to remember that some goods are very cheap. Rent is less than 5 percent of a worker's salary. Basic foods, such as bread, meat, and milk have maintained the same low prices for many years (the price of meat is two rubles per kilo just as it was 25 years ago). On the other hand, a car purchase requires two years' salary—even more for models like the popular "Zhiguli" ("Lada" on the Western markets). The main problem, however, is not the price of a car, but the shortage of available goods. Many people have saved the required two years' salary but must wait to buy a car.

Thus, the level of consumption remains low not because of the level of earnings but because of the poor supply of consumer goods. Thanks to a pricing policy that keeps the price of the "mass consumption goods" well under the production costs, the total amount of income exceeds the supply of goods on the market. Savings are high, amounting in 1984 to over 33 weeks of retail sales. There is no incentive to earn more in the form of bonuses or increased pay because there is little to buy.

Money does not provide access to goods—unless one is able to throw in really big money, the kind that can be used on the black market and in other forms of the "second economy." The second economy itself very often functions on a barter basis; goods are obtained in exchange for other goods or services. All this explains one of the "paradoxes of socialism": Even with empty shops one can get goods. In the West one often has the impression that there exists a privileged ruling class, with special shops and preferential access to all sorts of luxuries—well-furnished apartments, summer dachas, cars, and so on. Such privileges do exist. But the whole Soviet society is a network of interrelated opportunities to acquire some goods. Almost everybody has "entry" (according to the Russian expression, *vkhod*) to something. Entry might include being related to the cashier of a popular theater, knowing someone who has access to imported goods or to much needed spare parts for household appliances, etc. This indirect kind of purchasing is obviously very time-consuming and is one explanation for the lack of productivity in the enterprises.

To a certain extent, Soviet citizens are used to these conditions and find them normal. But they are complaining in letters to the newspapers that life is difficult because so much energy has to be expended to acquire the most common goods. Nevertheless, there is a general feeling of security, not only because jobs are secure, but also because of the extensive network of social services, albeit services of low quality. Standards of comparison with the outer world are available only to a minority. Western tourists travel only to big cities and some resorts. They present occasions for black marketeering to a limited number of Soviet citizens—those who buy jeans and foreign currency from tourists and make high profits out of their resale.

The average Soviet citizen never sees a tourist. Soviet citizens do travel in the other Eastern European countries, and here the comparison is sometimes staggeringly unfavorable. For instance, the sight of the Hungarian shops, or even the East German ones, is incredible for a Soviet visitor. But then the reaction is not, "Why can they achieve this when our system cannot?" but, "They are able to get all this just because we Soviets are subsidizing them."

In view of this state of affairs, the position of Gorbachev is, in principle, quite simple. He wants the Soviet worker to be more efficient, and to achieve this he has to improve the living standards so that there will be incentives for productivity. At the same time, he must foster a new morale in the struggle against the "lack of discipline," a term that includes sloth, absenteeism, and alcoholism.

Small steps are being taken in all directions. The first one, much publicized in the West, is the attempt to eradicate drunkenness, which has many economic and social consequences. Not only is the price of vodka being increased, but the consumption of hard liquor is being limited through a set of measures: No vodka is served in restaurants before 2:00 P.M., it can be sold in the shops only during a few hours of the day, and so on. The experiences of those countries that have implemented prohibition speak to the limits of such action. Vodka drinking is a social habit, largely linked with the unavailability of other sorts of consumer goods or leisure activities. Just recently an agreement was concluded with Coca-Cola—supplementing a similar one with Pepsi-Cola—to supply Soviet citizens with this popular soft drink, but the demand is much greater than the potential supply. With a general shortage in all types of recreation, vodka drinking remains the easiest one.

The authorities are, of course, aware of this. It is not by accident that one of the first moves made by Gorbachev was to adopt measures favorable to the "gardeners"—the urban workers who are allotted small plots of land on the outskirts of cities to grow fruit and vegetables and to raise poultry (these gardens are different from the private plots of the peasants, which are also encouraged). He has promised the Soviet citizens better repair services for apartments, better housing, and an improved telephone service.

Finally, Gorbachev is the first Soviet leader to admit publicly that some categories of citizens have particularly low living standards in the Soviet Union—families with many children and older, non-working people. He has committed himself to improvements in welfare benefits. This goal will probably be included in the social program now being prepared for the years 1986–2000 and to be announced at the 27th Party Congress in February 1986.

The question of the future of the Soviet economy is thus open. Many problems are facing Gorbachev, whose willingness to change is clear. The Soviet population is expecting changes, and their first impressions of the new leader have been favorable. The answer to the question of the economy's future lies largely outside the realm of economics and in the arena of domestic politics. But there is one other factor—the relationship of the Soviet economy to the outside world. Will economic relations with the outer world create additional constraints, or relax internal ones?

The outer world trade is important for the Soviet Union, but the USSR engages in trade on an *import-first* basis. It never felt, and does not now feel, a need to expand its foreign trade for the sake of exports. There are no autonomous individual firms trying to improve their competitive position through foreign markets. The domestic market is always large enough. Imports are planned in accordance with the basic needs of the economy; exports are adjusted to finance imports. The world energy crisis enabled the Soviet Union to cover most of its import requirements through energy exports. With the long-term decrease in the price of oil, beginning in 1983, things may change over time, but probably not dramatically. In any case, the decree of June 1985, as we have seen, provides incentives for the export of manufactured goods. This is due primarily to the desire to increase the technological potential of the manufacturing industry.

Because the Soviet Union is a huge and diversified country, the overall need for import goods as a share of domestic GNP is low. Imports amount to about 6 percent of GNP—a figure that has aroused some controversy among American scholars but seems reasonable enough. The corresponding figure for the United States is about 8 percent. The similarity ends there: The GNP of the U.S. is more than double the Soviet GNP, and the United States conducts its trade primarily with developed market economies, giving it a much greater impact on world trade.

The Soviet Union is, however, increasingly engaged in trade with the Western world. It now conducts about 56 percent of its trade with socialist countries (the figure for the 1970s was 65 percent); 13 percent with the developing (non-communist) countries (12 percent in 1970); and 31 percent with the market economies (23 percent in 1985). This pattern is quite stable. With the socialist countries, and particularly with Eastern Europe, the primary concern of the USSR is not expansion of trade but restoration of the balance of trade. Since 1975, when the price for Soviet oil supplied to Eastern Europe was substantially increased, the Soviet Union has maintained a surplus with its partners. This surplus is mostly expressed in a clearing currency (called the "transferable ruble"), so the Soviet Union cannot use this surplus in other markets. It is now pressing its partners for an increase in their exports to the Soviet Union. In particular, the Soviet Union is asking for more food and for more manufactured goods of a high quality. But this was expressed in June 1984 and little has happened. The balance has not been substantially altered.

Trade with the South (the Third World) also shows a substantial surplus, but in this case a significant part of it is expressed in hard currencies. More than 50 percent of Soviet exports are in arms sales (they appear in the Soviet trade statistics as a "residual," not-distributed among individual countries, but most of those sales are made to Middle East countries). On the import side, the Third World is an important supplier of food and especially grain (from Argentina and Brazil). These imports became important following the American grain embargo after the invasion of Afghanistan in December 1979. Oil is not a major item in Soviet imports from the Third World; but these countries are important to the Soviet Union as suppliers of some raw materials such as bauxite or phosphate rock.

The Soviet Union sees important advantages in trade with the West. It has restored its balance of trade with the West, after carrying a deficit in the mid-seventies. In fact, it is in surplus with the capitalist world in general. Even when it was in deficit, the Soviet Union did not develop an indebtedness as dramatic as that of its Eastern European neighbors. The credit squeeze directed against the USSR and Eastern Europe in 1982, as far as the USSR was concerned, was purely political (following the imposition of martial law in Poland). In addition, Western European banks were never really anxious to cut credit lines to the Soviet Union. Thus, the decrease in Soviet foreign borrowing in the years 1982–1983 really expresses the reluctance of the Soviet Union itself to borrow.

The present surplus of the Soviet Union with the West is not evenly distributed; it is spread widely over Western Europe. But there is a deficit with Japan and with North America. The reason for this lies in the structure of trade. The Soviet Union needs the Western technology and grain. If one regroups in the category "technology" both Western equipment and semi-finished goods, such as chemicals, tubes and other steel products, this category represents over 60 percent of the Soviet imports from the West. Food makes up about another 25 percent. These purchases are financed through energy sales, which now amount to 80 percent of the Soviet exports to the West.

The sales of energy products are primarily directed to Western Europe, but the imports of grain are mainly from North America (the United States and Canada), and the imports of technology are largely from Western Europe and Japan. The regional imbalance in trade is thus explained.

Finally, it is important to ask whether these patterns in Soviet trade will remain and whether they can be influenced by the West.

The food imports are, of course, related to the failure of Soviet agriculture, due both to inefficiency and to weather conditions. Since 1979, the Soviet Union has repeatedly experienced adverse climatic conditions; 1985 is probably the first "normal" year in many years. The management of agriculture may improve under the leadership of Gorbachev, who, after all, is a specialist in agriculture. The tremendous investment of resources in agriculture in accordance with the food program of 1982 may bring about some results; even a slight reduction in waste would reduce the need for imports. In any case, the situation is safe for the Soviet Union: The world grain market is sluggish, there are many suppliers, and the USSR is well aware of the U.S. interest in this trade—an interest demonstrated in the renewal of a long-term grain agreement in 1983, which includes a non-embargo clause.

The case for technology may be different. Here the U.S. government has engaged in a policy of export restrictions and sanctions aimed at limiting Soviet access to Western technology, particularly to technology that would enable it to expand its energy exports. This policy is questionable for two reasons. First, it hurts Western European interests (and also Japanese), and the 1982 "gas pipeline affair" was a cause of "acrimony" in the Western alliance. Second, Soviet dependency in this field is not firmly established. There are alternative suppliers; Eastern Europe, in particular the German Democratic Republic, is much more advanced in some areas of research and technological development than the Soviet Union. The Soviet Union itself has its own domestic technologies, though these are probably much less efficient than the Western ones. For instance, Soviet pipeline layers are much less powerful than U.S. Caterpillars. Until very recently, Soviet industry did not produce tubes of 56" diameter. This meant that for the Euro-Siberian pipeline they would have had to use two smaller tubes instead of one. Drastic reductions in Western sales to the Soviet Union would probably cause lags and bottlenecks, but they would not stop the technical progress in the Soviet Union. They might even spur it, as the long history of embargoes shows.

Turning to the export side, the question really is, Can the Soviet Union expand its energy production and then find the necessary outlets? The first part of the question can probably be answered positively. True, oil production has been slowly declining since the end of 1983, but the oil fields are very poorly managed and production may increase just by better management. New fields are to be explored in Siberia (albeit at high costs). Gas production is also expanding beyond the expectations of the plans. But what about the market? Western Europe is sure to remain a good market, and the demand may even rise with the recovery of these economies. Other suppliers are available, but since the exhaustion of the Dutch fields, the Soviet Union is a cheaper supplier for gas than any other and—whether for oil or for gas—it is arguably a safer bet than Middle East or African exporters, particularly in the context of a sound supply diversification policy.

It appears, then, that these trends in Soviet trade are stable. The Soviet Union may go on using the foreign trade sector as it has before. The experience of the years 1982 and 1983 has shown that even in a tense international context, business has gone on almost as usual with the Western world. But this business is very "primitive" in its pattern: energy and raw materials for manufactures and food. The Soviet Union is not really engaged in the international division of labor. Here political trade restrictions may indeed make the difference. Because of Western trade restrictions, the Soviet Union cannot be involved in industrial cooperation programs that imply access to high technology. The development of a sophisticated machine-building export industry is unlikely because of the lack of domestic incentives and because the Soviet Union does not really need this for export as long as it can sell energy. Consequently, the impulse has to come from inside—which brings us full circle to the uncertainties of economic reform under Gorbachev.

SCIENCE AND TECHNOLOGY IN THE SOVIET UNION: HISTORICAL BACKGROUND AND CONTEMPORARY PROBLEMS

Vladimir Krinsky, 1922

KENDALL E. BAILES

mong the most popular works still produced in the Soviet Union is a play by the nineteenth-century writer Ostrovsky. Entitled *The Thunderstorm*, it portrays the conflict between the traditional culture of Russia and the striving of many Russian young people for more freedom and for a more rational culture. The thunderstorm of the title is both real and symbolic of the state of mind of the leading characters. It sets the mood of the play, which involves a personal tragedy resulting from the clash between the traditional, religious bonds of family life and the scientific and more libertarian views that had begun to penetrate provincial Russian society in the last half of the nineteenth century.

Throughout the play, a minor character appears who comments on the action and places it in context. He is identified as a self-taught mechanic, a man who represents the new scientific and technological view of life. His beliefs are juxtaposed to the beliefs of the traditional culture. When asked to explain what causes the approaching thunderstorm, which the superstitious believe to be a sign of God's anger and a warning of punishment for personal sins, the self-taught mechanic replies that it is simply electricity, really nothing to be feared and in fact more beneficial than harmful.

We don't know how many such self-educated new Russian men

and women there were in the late nineteenth century whose views were shaped by modern scientific ideas about nature and about mankind's place in nature. What we can say is that modern scientific and technological attitudes spread rapidly among the population of Russia after the early 1860s, and that science gradually ceased to be a monopoly of the nobility and of foreign experts in the Imperial Russian Academy of Sciences and a few universities, as it had been in the eighteenth and early nineteenth centuries. The revolutionaries and the radical intelligentsia who came to power in 1917 gave science and technology a central place in their own ideology. In rebellion against traditional Russian culture with its strong religious values, they raised science almost to a substitute religion by their strong belief in propagating scientific knowledge as an antidote for Russia's ancient ills. Since the establishment of the Soviet system, this has hardened into what we might call today the "scientism" of the regime, with its optimistic view of the potential of modern science and technology for unlimited good, and its rejection of all religiously oriented viewpoints and attempts to reconcile science with religion.

In the years between the emancipation of the serfs in 1861 and the Russian revolutions of 1917, Russia produced a small but world-famous group of academic scientists—people like Mendeleev, Pavlov, Mechnikov, Sechenov, the Kabalevskys, and others. Most of these academic scientists, who numbered no more than several thousand at the time of the 1897 census, were drawn from the established, traditional classes of Russia. More than 80 percent were from the hereditary nobility; the remainder were largely children of Russian orthodox clergy and middle-class professionals. Professional careers in science, which almost always included an expensive period in Western Europe before returning to a professorship or research position in the imperial government, were open mostly to the members of these classes, who represented the top 2 or 3 percent of the Russian population as a whole. The tsarist government deliberately tried to restrict higher education of this type to members of such classes, in the hope that they would prove more loyal to the autocratic system.

But in fact the people most attracted to professional careers in science tended to be the poorer and more discontented members of such groups, the children of middle and poorer nobility who no longer could or wanted to make a living from their landed estates— if they owned land at all. Or such scientists came from the children of the clergy, who could not enter that overcrowded profession, or who no longer believed in the theological view of the universe put forward by a state church which preached obedience, humility, and the sin of trying to understand rationally the mysteries of God's universe.

The result was that many who entered science in this period were like the angry young man, Bazarov, portrayed in Turgenev's famous novel of the 1860s, *Fathers and Sons*. Coming from declining classes, ashamed of a Russia so backward materially when compared with Western Europe, they sought in science a new role for themselves: to save their country and help humanity through science and its applications. Few of them were in favor of violent revolution but most were highly critical of the status quo and many were in favor of liberal parliamentary systems. Their fierce belief in the positive values of science and modern secular education made them strongly sympathetic to the lower classes, whom they sought to help and among whom they tried to spread a scientific world view. Many of them put great effort into extending education through mass literacy, popular scientific journalism, correspondence and night school courses for workers and for women, who were excluded from the universities and other state-sponsored higher education.

The activity of such scientists helped to popularize scientific attitudes and educational work among a much wider element of the population. It has often been said that the small community of Russian scientists before 1917 were largely interested in basic, theoretical science and not in applied science, that they were bookworms and laboratory recluses; this in fact is not really true. While some were brilliant theoreticians and innovators in basic science, many chose their specialities for their direct bearing on Russia's problems. The chemist Mendeleev, for example, worked closely with the Russian defense establishment to aid Russia's technically backward military forces. To help restore the fertility of Russia's overcrowded and exhausted central agricultural regions, Dokuchaev pioneered the scientific study of soils. Mechnikov pioneered the study of immunity from disease to help cope with the plagues of cholera, typhus, and other diseases that periodically ravaged the Russian countryside. A desire to raise the productivity of Russian agriculture and help combat the famines that were another plague of Russian life led Timiriazev to pioneer the study of plant physiology. Vernadsky did pioneering work in mineralogy and geochemistry, in part as a way of helping locate the strategic raw materials necessary for Russian industrialization and national strength.

Such scientists helped in the prerevolutionary era to set the trend for combining theory with practice, which the Soviets, and Stalin in particular, turned into the basic pattern of Soviet science for many decades. This community of scientists, in other words, provided the basis for Soviet science after the Revolution. Very few of Russia's scientists emigrated after the Revolution; the large majority remained, despite frequent disagreements with the Soviet regime, and dominated most of Russian science intellectually for several decades after 1917.

Most Russian professional scientists before 1917 were liberal and critical of the tsarist government, and many of them welcomed the first Russian revolution in February of 1917, which overthrew the Romanov dynasty. They hoped for the establishment of a liberal parliamentary government and supported the Provisional Government of 1917. The overthrow of that government by the Bolsheviks in October of 1917 was opposed by the majority of well-known professional scientists. In the 1920s the Academy of Sciences, which was responsible for training many professional scientists and for coordinating research in the basic theoretical sciences, became a center of opposition to government control. Under pressure from Stalin and the Communist Party, the Academy lost its autonomy in the late 1920s and was flooded with new members of two types—Marxist theoreticians and engineers. A Department of Technical Sciences was set up, which soon became the largest in the Academy, while Communist Party members assumed control over the planning of science.

With the Communist takeover of the Academy came a great expansion of professional science in the Soviet Union. Professional scientists involved in research work increased from less than 3000 in 1897 to more than one million today. In fact, in recent years the Soviet Union has boasted the largest community of professional research scientists anywhere in the world, including the United States. Who were these new scientists and what was their role in Soviet society? Between 1928 and 1935 high quotas for entrance into higher education were established for industrial workers and poor peasants and their children in an attempt to proletarianize science. In 1935, however, such quotas were abolished as ineffective and entrance was based on merit, as measured by competitive examinations, and political reliability, as measured by Party affiliation. These remain the principal means of recruitment to scientific careers today. For example, 50 percent of all

Soviet scientists with graduate degrees today are Communist Party members, compared to about 2 percent in 1928.

In fact, science has one of the highest percentages of Party members of any professional group in the USSR. Their high Party saturation is not reflected in the number of professional scientists in major Party and government positions. Instead, important scientists tend to have influence as consultants to top Party and government leaders, who themselves tend to be technologists by education, that is, graduate engineers or agronomists. (Some 75 to 80 percent of the Politburo in recent years have a background in engineering or agronomy, including Gorbachev and his three recent appointees to that body. About two-thirds of the Central Committee have a similar background. Only about 5 percent of the Central Committee are professional scientists, and there are no professional scientists in the Politburo.) For example, when Gorbachev went to Great Britain shortly before Chernenko's death, he was accompanied by a man named Yevgeny Velikhov. Velikhov is a full member of the Academy of Sciences and is one of the most important Soviet specialists on lasers (and probably, by implication, on "Star Wars" technology). He is also the man who recently organized a new section in the Academy of Sciences devoted to fundamental research in computer technology and automation. Approximately Gorbachev's age, Velikhov represents a younger generation in Soviet science who are becoming advisors to the top political leadership.

While opportunity to enter the sciences as professionals has been widened under the Soviet system as compared with the tsarist system, statistics show that the large majority of all younger Soviet scientists today come from families of the intelligentsia and white-collar classes, a group which makes up only about one-quarter of the population. The intelligentsia and the "bosses" (professional and managerial groups) in particular have been successful at promoting their children, thus reproducing their class. These are the families that instill both the motivation and the cultural background for excelling. In addition, they tend to have the money to hire tutors for their children and to supplement the inadequate state scholarships provided to all students in higher education—and they often have the connections to get their children into the best schools. Since the 1930s, therefore, careers in science have tended to become more the domain of the Soviet upper and middle classes, just as they were in the tsarist period. In fact, it is not uncommon to find children following in the footsteps of their parents in the same or a closely related specialty.

Careers in science also tend often to attract people who are more dissident or at least more critical of the status quo than, say, the majority of engineers or the majority of industrial workers. When dissidence was becoming popular in the late 1950s and early 1960s, until it was crushed or at least driven deeper underground by Andropov as KGB (Secret Police) chief after 1966, a large percentage of the dissidents—people who signed petitions and wrote dissident literature—came from research institutes and universities. A large portion of them were in the natural sciences and technological research. This fact tends to support a belief that the critical tradition of the Russian scientific intelligentsia has not entirely died out but is kept alive, particularly among the best educated sectors of the population, such as those engaged in research positions. It is difficult to know how deeply the roots of such dissidence go, but there is little doubt that it still survives.

So long as professional science continues to grow in the Soviet Union, opportunities will remain for well-qualified and motivated young people from all walks of life to enter those professions. However, in the last decade or so, such growth has slowed, leading to signs of increased frustration and slower mobility for those Soviet young people—especially those from worker and peasant backgrounds—who hope to enter and to rise in such professions. This promises to constitute an important problem for the Gorbachev leadership in the area of social policy. The sciences for many years have had the highest career prestige in Soviet society, higher than political work, with physics at the top of all such recent public opinion surveys. One reason may be that a career in science is viewed as far more secure than political work. Once you have a degree and a research job in Soviet science it is virtually impossible to be fired—except for political dissent. This leads to great security and stability for Soviet research organizations, but also to an increased sense of "arterial sclerosis" in the research and development sector of the economy. The situation is particularly frustrating for those who would like to see more innovation and greater opportunities for those who demonstrate an ability for innovation.

While science has received great moral and financial support from the Soviet state for the last sixty or so years, it has not been nearly as creative as one would expect from a community that today includes between one-quarter and one-third of all the highly qualified research workers in the world. The USSR spends as much as the United States on science, but its scientists publish only half as much. Measured both in terms of world recognition, such as Nobel Prizes, and in the quantity and quality of original research published, Soviet science has clearly been less productive than science in the major countries of the West—a fact that the Soviet press itself recognizes and has discussed extensively over the past fifteen to twenty years. For example, since 1953, the Soviet Union has received only five Nobel Prizes in physics and chemistry, compared to thirty-eight for the United States. Although the Soviet Union publishes about 20 percent of all the scientific articles published annually in the world, citations of Soviet articles amount to only 3 to 4 per cent of the number of citations of scientific literature by scientists of other countries.

In contrast, the United States and Britain annually publish 55 percent of all scientific articles and gather about 55 percent of all citations by foreign scientists. In very few areas do the Soviets stand at the cutting edge of world science. While the reasons for this are not entirely clear, I can suggest at least two possibilities: For many years during the period of rapid modernization—the 1930s to the 1950s—Soviet science was largely harnessed to industrialization, to increasing modern education, and to absorbing the scientific legacy of the West. Such work was by its nature imitative rather than highly creative.

The second reason may, however, be more fundamental; that is the extreme centralization and bureaucratization of Soviet science. Joseph Ben-David in his book, *The Role of the Scientist in Society*, suggests that the most centralized systems of scientific organization have been the least creative historically. He uses France and Russia as his examples. The most decentralized and autonomous, i.e., where scientists themselves play a primary role in the making of science policy and where the resources for research are varied, have been the most productive. He sees Britain and the United States at this end of the spectrum. His generalization is controversial, but it is certainly worth consideration.

What we can say with certainty is that Soviet science is characterized by a high degree of centralization and by many layers of bureaucracy. Whereas until 1961 the Academy of Sciences supervised most scientific research, in 1961 a new State Committee for Science and Technology usurped part of that role in applied science.

The Soviet Academy of Sciences remains responsible for supervising and coordinating most fundamental or basic research in the USSR. The State Committee is something like a ministry for research and development, with particular concern for defense-related research. It operates under the Council of Ministers of the Soviet government and handles budgets and planning for Soviet research and development in the area of applied science and technological innovation. It has always been headed by Party members who are also closely associated with the defense industry. It must also work in close co-ordination with the State Planning Commission (Gosplan) and the Communist Party's Department for Science and Higher Education.

The State Committee approves research plans, allocates money, and checks on the results of applied research conducted by the USSR Academy of Sciences, the local academies of science in the Soviet republics, and research institutes in industry, medicine, and agriculture. This system may be effective in focusing work on those areas of most interest to Soviet leaders in the Politburo—such as defense and the space program—but one wonders how much support and how many risks planners in the State Committee may be willing to undertake to advance the more esoteric frontiers of applied science.

Obtaining support is certainly a problem for pioneering scientists and inventors in every society, but the monopoly control of science exercised in the Soviet system may help to hold down the innovators. Whether this is good or bad for society and culture as a whole is, of course, another question. Critics of modern science and technology in the West have generally felt that the pace of change has sometimes been too rapid, without adequate concern for its effects on society and the natural environment. But Soviet leaders under both Brezhnev and Gorbachev, in their rhetoric at least, view the slow pace of Soviet innovation in science and technology as a definite problem and continue to discuss it extensively in the press.

Soviet leaders no longer claim, as Stalinist leaders did right after World War II, that the Russians invented and discovered virtually everything worthwhile in science and technology. One Soviet comedian parodied that outdated attitude in the following way: An American visitor to Moscow during the Stalin era was perplexed by hearing everywhere about the two great Russian scientists and inventors, Orlov and Stavrov. The American started making inquiries about Orlov, for it was said that he had not only discovered the North and South Poles, but had invented the telephone, the telegraph, the printing press, the electric light, the steam engine, the internal combustion engine, and indoor plumbing. Everyone seemed to agree that Orlov invented all of these things, but he was said to be only the second greatest Russian scientist and inventor. "But then who was the greatest scientist and inventor?" the American asked, naively. "Why, that was Stavrov," he was told. "What did he invent?" the American inquired. "Oh," came the answer, "he invented Orlov."

In that anecdote rests one of the major dilemmas of Soviet society, both in the recent past and in the Gorbachev era: the gap between the claims of Soviet advances in science and technology and the realities of a society that, compared with the West and Japan, remains backward in most such areas. Surplus labor supplies from the countryside have been exhausted, and most adults are already working. Surplus laborers provided the source of much Soviet growth in the past, but now science and technology are the key to continued economic growth. Yet economic growth has slowed from about 5 percent a year in the 1960s to 2 percent today. The major cause of this slowdown is a decline in the rate of productivity increase, that is, the efficiency with which each employed person produces goods and services. The typical attitude is summed up in the popular saying, "Since they only pretend to pay us, we only pretend to work."

More rapid economic growth is essential if the Soviet leadership is to meet its goals of catching up with the West economically. In fact, one of the real dangers for the Soviet Union today is that Japan, which is now the third largest economy in the world, will catch up with and surpass the Soviet Union in the next few years. If this happens, it would be a major humiliation for the Soviet Union, nearly as important, I think, as the defeat of Russia by Japan in 1905—a military defeat that sent shock waves through the Russian Empire. An economic defeat of the Soviet Union by Japan would probably send similar shock waves through the Soviet leadership, if not through the population as a whole (though the present government controls the population more tightly than the tsar did in 1905). Japan, after all, is a nation with less than half the population of the Soviet Union and has no natural resources to boast of, except for its highly skilled and resourceful population. Since both nations began their emergence from a traditional economic and social system at approximately the same time—in the 1860s—a rapidly growing Japan that may surpass an increasingly sluggish Soviet Union in the near future would dramatize the failures of the Soviet system, much as the defeats at Port

Arthur, Mukden, and Tsushima in 1904–1905 dramatized the failures of tsarist Russia.

The remedy for the slowdown in economic growth, as Soviet economists see it, is better applied science and technology—for example, the wide-scale application of computers, greater automation through the use of robotics, etc., and more efficient forms of organization, including better material incentives for improved work performance. Yet the Soviet system is very poorly organized to encourage the development of automation and computerization on which the most advanced economies in the world today depend for much of their growth. The Soviets have been relatively successful at copying and adapting computer *hardware* from the West and Japan, but their lack of innovation and their dependence on the West and Japan for hardware has kept them five to ten years behind in this vital area. Their real weakness, however, lies in the area of software and service, and in their fear of the freer flow of information that computers would make possible.

In the West, starting from a well-developed business machines industry, like IBM and Burroughs, which the Soviet Union lacked and still lacks, the computer industry developed rapidly from spin-off companies begun by entrepreneurs who were willing to take risks and who provided a high degree of service to their customers. These nonconformists profited from a system in which a free flow of information was encouraged and risk-taking was not so heavily penalized. Software companies in particular did not require a high degree of capital and were free to develop the innovative techniques upon which the computerization of Western societies has proceeded, raising labor productivity to new highs.

The Soviet Union, on the other hand, has an economy of huge monopolistic organizations—huge organizations that do not respond quickly to challenges and the need to change. And it has a political system that has been very suspicious of the free flow of information that computer technology requires for its development—and which it facilitates through personal computers, computer networking, rapid data storage, retrieval, and dissemination. In a society that controls and licenses even ditto machines and other copiers, one can imagine the nightmares that KGB officers and Politburo members suffer at the thought of a society of computer hackers, personal computers in the home, modems, and high speed printers. *Samizdat*, i.e., underground publications, would spread like wild fire through such a society and would threaten the tightly controlled and well-developed system of censorship. Yet the dilemma is that the long-range economic growth of the USSR and perhaps even its military security may increasingly depend upon the development of a computer-based society.

There are several alternatives, besides the status quo, available to the Gorbachev leadership. One is to try to make a centralized and bureaucratic economy work more efficiently, through better incentives, better communication, and tighter controls. Another alternative is to create a more decentralized economy based on market socialism, that is, a mixed economy that permits some private enterprise and encourages competition, both domestically and with foreign companies. More competition in the economy, including more competition in science and in the area of technological innovation, has been recommended sporadically by Soviet economists, but so far the Gorbachev leadership seems to have ruled out anything approaching the reforms that have taken place in Hungary and China—that is, market socialism, or a return to something resembling the mixed economy of the NEP (New Economic Policy) era in the Soviet Union itself during the 1920s.

To date, the Gorbachev leadership seems to have rejected any experiments with market socialism. But if such experiments succeed in other communist countries, particularly in a large country like China, that would greatly increase the internal pressure on the Soviet leadership to consider such measures. The Chinese experiment in the economy has been accompanied by an experiment in research institutes, in the universities, and in higher education—that is, giving them more autonomy, allowing freer discussion in scientific debates, and building up the status of intellectuals and experts in Chinese society. Of course, no ruling communist party can afford to say it is reverting to a system resembling the West or Japan; and even China, very likely, will remain a single-party, communist state for a long time to come. But if most of the communist world does return to a NEP-like mixed economy, with extensive competition and somewhat greater intellectual freedom built into it, then the pressure on the Soviet Communist Party to do likewise will increase immeasurably. The quality of Soviet science and technology, not to mention the quality of life in the Soviet Union, may well depend on such developments.

THE SOVIET NATIONALITY QUESTION

El Lissitzky, Symbol of unity of republics within the Soviet Union

G A I L   W.   L A P I D U S

The management of relations among its diverse national groups is a major challenge for the Soviet system. As events of recent years have made clear, the Soviet Union is not immune to what is essentially a worldwide phenomenon—an upsurge of ethnic and national consciousness. From the Baltic States to Soviet Central Asia, the Soviet system faces competing claims to resources, power, and status.

That rising ethno-nationalism is one of the most serious problems facing the Soviet Union today is a view widely shared by specialists on the Soviet Union. Indeed, some would go so far as to assert that it is the single most serious problem confronting the system in the years ahead, and a few would argue that it is likely to prove unmanageable over the long run. Such eminent specialists as Zbigniew Brzezinski and Richard Pipes, for example, have predicted that the Soviet Union could well fragment along the lines of its national republics, and some have suggested that this could actually happen within the next twenty years.

The Soviet leadership would not share that judgment. They nonetheless clearly recognize that the management of "national relations" is one of the most important as well as one of the most delicate problems on their political agenda, with profound implications for the long-term stability and legitimacy of the Soviet system.

To assess properly the nature of this problem and its likely impact on the Soviet future, it is important to bring a historical and comparative perspective to the Soviet scene. We need to explore the conditions under which national grievances or national tensions are mobilized into politically salient movements and the extent to which such conditions are present, or potentially present, in the Soviet Union today. This broader question in turn suggests three topics on which I would like to focus. First, what have been the main features of the Soviet strategy for managing a multinational empire and how successful has that strategy been? Second, what are the major tensions and problems that Soviet policymakers are now obliged to address? Finally, how likely is the Soviet system to manage these problems, and what impact are they likely to have on the long-term legitimacy and viability of the Soviet system?

Let me begin by stating that the Soviet Union is one of the most complex multinational states in the world today, comprising over one hundred different nations and nationalities, of which twenty have a population of over one million. It is also one in which geography is a critical factor. Western journalistic writings all too often use the terms "Russia" and "the Soviet Union" interchangeably, when, in fact, they are quite distinct. A Russian heartland, which extends from the western part of the Soviet Union all the way across Siberia to the Pacific Ocean, is surrounded by a number of non-Russian republics that form a large part of the Soviet Union's external borders. From the Baltic States, with their proximity to Scandinavia and Poland, to the Ukraine, which borders on Eastern Europe, down to the Transcaucasus and Soviet Central Asia, along the borders of Turkey, Afghanistan, and the Middle East, the non-Russian republics form a rather vulnerable and insecure periphery. They represent in effect both a barrier and a buffer to outside influences and, conceivably, to outside armies that might seek to penetrate the Russian heartland.

The composition of the Soviet population also distinguishes it from the many other multinational systems in which two major groups dominate the political arena. Russians, with 52 percent of the total population, constitute a very slight majority. If you add to this figure the two other Slavic nationalities—the Ukrainians and the Byelorussians—you account for roughly 75 percent of the Soviet population. The remaining quarter includes the largely Muslim Central Asian populations, the Georgians and Armenians, and the three Baltic nations of Estonia, Latvia, and Lithuania, which taken together comprise only a tiny part of the Soviet population.

All too often accounts of Soviet nationality problems conjure up images of a struggle between the Russians and the non-Russians, two large and cohesive groups pitted against each other. It is important to bear in mind that the non-Russian nationalities are themselves extremely diverse. They encompass all conceivable levels of socio-economic development, from the highly industrialized and very Westernized parts of the Baltic to the largely agricultural, rural, and comparatively underdeveloped regions of Central Asia. This diversity of socio-economic development is accompanied by a diversity of cultures, of languages, and of religious traditions. For example, Russian Orthodoxy retains some vitality in the Russian Republic; Roman Catholicism plays a significant role in Lithuania; and Islamic practices remain widespread in Soviet Central Asia.

Diversity is evident, finally, in patterns of historical relationships to Russia. For some nationalities, Russia has traditionally been a protector against other enemies, as in the case of the Armenians against the Turks. For others it is Russia itself that is the traditional threat. Far from being a cohesive and anti-Russian force, the non-Russian populations are fragmented and often at odds.

How then, we may ask, has the Soviet system managed this enormously complex set of relationships over the years? It was Lenin himself who in the early years of the Soviet regime elaborated a strategy for dealing with the nationality problem, a strategy whose essential features have not changed since then. In 1917 Lenin faced the shattered legacy of the Russian Empire. In the chaos and disorganization of World War I, many of the nationalities that had been incorporated into the empire under the tsars had seized the opportunity to secede and form independent states. As a socialist, Lenin genuinely believed that nations and nationalism were but transitional phenomena in human history and that a classless society would also be one without national antagonisms. As a political strategist, however, Lenin sought to use powerful sentiments on behalf of the revolutionary cause.

What Lenin and Stalin succeeded in doing was to reconstitute that old Russian Empire, to draw those nations back, forcibly if necessary, into the fabric of the new Soviet state. But they did so by creating, in effect, a nominal federal system in which a high degree of economic and political centralization, exercised through a unitary party, was combined with limited local (and largely cultural) autonomy for the major national groups, which were organized as republics.

Imagine how the United States might look if it were organized as the Soviet Union is. Imagine, if you will, a federal system in which the major political and administrative boundaries are also ethnic boundaries. The state of California might then well be a Chicano state; New York, a Jewish state; Illinois, a Polish state; Alabama, a black state. Imagine, too, that instead of being largely composed of immigrant communities dispersed throughout the country, each of these states represented an historic national homeland in which that dominant nationality or ethnic group had lived for many centuries.

Paradoxically, by opting for this approach, the founders of the Soviet state created, in effect, a series of mini nation-states. Because the political and administrative boundaries of the Soviet republics coincided, by and large, with ethnic boundaries, the two tended to reinforce each other, providing a framework for asserting the interests and demands of the particular ethnic groups.

The Soviet leadership has, by and large, managed the nationality problem through a combination of rapid modernization, coercion, and political cooptation. First, Stalin largely destroyed the traditional elites of the non-Russian regions as well as the traditional bases of their social, economic, and political power; he used economic development to bring into being from within those minority nationalities new elites loyal to the Soviet system and with a stake in Soviet rule. The more coercive aspects of Soviet nationality policy have diminished in recent years but are still evoked against any national leaders or groups with aspirations to secession or greater autonomy.

The result of this entire strategy, which differs in some very important respects from that of classical colonial sytems, has been to build a fundamental tension into Soviet nationality policy. On the one hand, nations and nationalities are recognized as fundamental social units—in contrast with the United States, where citizenship is the fundamental category and ethnicity is largely self-ascribed. For example, in the passport that every Soviet citizen is obliged to carry, his or her nationality is specifically inscribed, either as given by birth or, in the case of children of mixed marriages, selected at age eighteen from the two—the nationalities of the mother and father.

Because national identity is recognized as a fundamental fact of political organization, Soviet policy has also resulted to some degree in the development of national languages, educations, and cultures. Those who have traveled in the non-Russian republics of the Soviet Union—Armenia, for example—will no doubt remember that primary and secondary schools are conducted in Armenian, the street signs are written in Armenian, Armenian language newspapers exist alongside Russian ones, and radio and television programs are broadcast in Armenian as well as Russian. In short, the republics provide a framework for the assertion and protection of group identity, interests, and values.

At the same time, this pluralist aspect of Soviet nationality policy is in fundamental tension with the centralizing and Russifying impulse. Russians form the core population of the USSR, concentrated not only in the Russian Republic but also in the key cities of the non-Russian republics; Russian is the language of communication among republics and its study is compulsory. These facts tend to give Russian culture a preeminent place.

Moreover, although elites of the local nationality play a visible and important role in governing their own republics, at the center of the Soviet sytem the key elites—Party, military, economic—tend to be Russian or Slavic.

The tension between the multinational and pluralist aspects of Soviet policy and its centralizing and assimilationist thrust is also reflected in Soviet ideology, which combines a commitment to the "flowering" of national cultures with the conviction that a process of convergence and rapprochement will result in a society in which national antagonisms and differences will disappear.

The central problem in Soviet nationality policy is to maintain the delicate balance between these two elements: to assure the continued dominance of the Russian majority and of its values, language, and cultural heritage, and at the same time to reduce the alienation of non-Russian nationalities, many of whom suffered oppression and discrimination under tsarist rule, and to guarantee that they will be equal, valued, and respected members of a Soviet multinational community.

In practice, Soviet policy has fluctuated between these impulses. But even the most skillful leadership confronts a constant tug of war over the broad thrust of that policy. This tug of war is visible across a whole range of very practical issues. To take one example, there is

"GORBACHEV'S GONE TOO FAR!"

the problem of managing a federal system. Centralizing and unifying pressures coming from Moscow conflict with the desire of republics to adapt central policies to local conditions and needs, or to maintain and assert their own autonomy. The question of whether this federal system represents a temporary, tactical compromise on the path to a unitary system, or whether Lenin intended it to be a long-term and permanent solution, is still a subject of debate. For example, in the discussions surrounding the new constitution of 1977, proposals to abolish the national republics were reported to have been rejected.

A second tug of war involves resource allocation as the different republics and regions of the Soviet Union compete over the division of the national economic pie. The less developed republics remind the leadership of its commitment to social and economic equalization and request greater resources for development, particularly in view of their surplus labor—the result of rapid population growth.

The more developed republics complain that they make a disproportionate contribution to national wealth and receive less in return than others. They argue that in view of their highly skilled manpower, developed infrastructure, low transportation costs, and proximity to Europe, the high returns on investment in their region warrant a larger share.

Although lobbying is not the highly organized activity in Moscow that it is in Washington, the process of central economic planning involves enormous tugging and bargaining behind the scenes. A Siberian "lobby," for example, points to its vast resources of untapped mineral wealth, oil, gas, and other natural resources, as well as its strategic location, to support its claim to a larger investment in building up the economy of that region.

Nationality issues also come very much to the forefront with regard to demographic trends. The Soviet leadership would clearly welcome more rapid population growth to alleviate manpower shortages, to promote economic growth, and perhaps to increase its pool of military manpower. It would especially like to encourage larger families among the Russian population of the Soviet Union and to reduce family size among the Muslim populations of Soviet Central Asia. This is obviously so sensitive an issue that to argue it openly is difficult, but some Central Asian demographers have in effect suggested that a differential population policy is inherently discriminatory.

Yet another source of tension between various national groups stems from competition over upward mobility and the access to higher education and desirable jobs on which it depends. In the larger cities of a republic like Uzbekistan, to take one example, there are very substantial Russian settler communities, many of them going back to the nineteenth century, when Russian colonists moved in to develop these outlying areas. For decades they constituted a political, economic, and managerial elite—and an instrument of central control over the republics. At the same time, economic development and the expansion of educational opportunities created in Uzbekistan, as in other republics, a very substantial indigenous elite, which by now has relatively high educational qualifications and wants to see its own children occupy these positions.

Competing claims to educational and occupational preferment occasionally find expression in arguments over whether native nationalities should receive preferential treatment in access to schools and jobs. Similar issues are at stake in language policy. The question of whether Uzbek or Russian will be used in the state and Party bureaucracy, in research institutes, and in journals, has direct implications for the career choices and life chances of young people of different nationalities. Conflict over the language in which television programs will be broadcast, books published, classes taught, and theatrical productions performed is another aspect of the struggle among competing national elites to shape their futures. During an earlier period of rapid economic development, ample opportunities for upward mobility minimized the areas of potential ethnic conflict.

As economic growth slows, as social development stabilizes, and as the whole system of social stratification crystallizes and hardens and competition becomes sharper, frustration over disappointed expectations can easily fuse with national antagonisms. Thus what may appear to be symbolic issues, involving the status of one's national language, culture, and history are in fact issues that affect careers and material interests as well.

Finally, the nationality problem also affects the interaction of domestic and foreign policy. Here the case of Central Asia is especially interesting. Beginning in the Khrushchev period, the Soviets have made a very deliberate effort, as part of their overtures to the Third World, to present the Soviet Union as a model for the successful development of backward societies emerging from the struggle for national liberation against colonial oppression. They have sought to portray Central Asia as an example of what other Third World countries might accomplish by turning to a socialist path: A once backward, underdeveloped, illiterate, and impoverished region is now endowed with a modern industrial sector, a developed social infrastructure, high rates of literacy, and visible cultural achievement. Tashkent, the capital of Uzbekistan, figures prominently as a showcase and meeting place in Soviet political and cultural diplomacy in the Third World and in Soviet relations with Asia, Africa, and the Middle East.

This effort has double-edged consequences: It gives Central Asia growing importance and visibility in the Soviet system and Central Asians a broader role in diplomatic, technical, and cultural exchanges. Increased visibility in turn provokes wider claims for constructing conference centers or refurbishing historical monuments. It also has the effect of opening Central Asia to foreign influences to a greater degree, much as the process of detente somewhat reduced the insulation of Moscow from the West. Thus the effort to project Soviet influence into the Third World also makes the Soviet Union, and this region in particular, more vulnerable to external influences.

The scope and nature of this vulnerability is a major question, especially with the rise of Islamic fundamentalism in Iran and the Soviet military intervention in Afghanistan. However, the argument that the Soviet invasion of Afghanistan was intended to prevent the spread of Islamic fundamentalism across Soviet borders has a serious flaw: It would argue more for an effort to seal that border and reduce the level of interaction between Central Asia and Afghanistan. By sending not only troops but large numbers of advisors to Afghanistan to rebuild its governmental and security apparatus, reorganize its economy, and transform its school system, the Soviet leadership is demonstrating a confidence in the long-term transformation of Afghanistan rather than a fear of contagion. The invasion of Afghanistan was the outcome of a whole sequence of policy decisions in which concern about the spread of Islamic fundamentalism need not be assumed to have played a central role. Moreover, there is little evidence of any serious spillover of Islamic fundamentalism from Iran and Afghanistan to Central Asia, and good reason to believe that the political, economic, and social environment of the region is extremely inhospitable to its development. This is not to suggest that the Soviet leadership has no reason for concern; indeed, it will typically over-insure itself against any conceivable threat and combat any potentially subversive influence.

While much of the discussion of Soviet nationality problems focuses on the rising national consciousness of the non-Russian groups within the Soviet Union and their efforts to claim a greater share of power and resources, it is also important to bear in mind that rising Russian nationalism is part of this overall picture. The claims or grievances of Uzbeks or Armenians or Estonians have provoked a defensive reaction on the part of Russians themselves. We are seeing the emergence of what might be described as a Russian nationalist political sentiment—opposed to the massive transfer of resources from the Russian heartland to the outlying republics, anxious about current demographic trends, eager for policies which will encourage high birth rates in the Russian territories, critical of affirmative action on behalf of other nationalities, perceiving Russians to be the victims of discrimination, and concerned with the preservation of Russian historical and national traditions in the face of rapid modernization. A growing body of literature laments the wanton destruction of the Russian natural environment, as well as of its historical and cultural environment—from Lake Baikal to lovely old churches, in a spectrum of opinions ranging from the desire for a cultural renaissance to an extreme and even xenophobic political nationalism.

Looking ahead, then, to the long-term implications of these problems, what are the prospects that this rising national consciousness and self-assertiveness is likely to lead to serious cleavages, potential secessionist movements, and, indeed, to the possible disintegration of the Soviet system? I would suggest that the trends I have been discussing create genuine and important problems of political management. They will require bargaining within the system and continuing readjustments in traditional institutions and policies, but, given skillful political leadership, these problems are not intrinsically unmanageable. They can be addressed in a variety of ways short of the breakup of the Soviet system itself.

Several factors contribute to making the problems relatively manageable. First of all, there are many obstacles to the emergence of nationalist political movements within the Soviet Union, just as there are to the organization of any spontaneous, unofficial movements within the Soviet system. Efforts to organize a dissident movement, a feminist movement, a workers' movement, a peace movement, have all been shattered.

Not only does the Soviet regime have exceptionally powerful mechanisms of coercion available to it; it is also in a position to proffer carrots as well as sticks. The elites of the national republics have considerable incentive to work within the system rather than to oppose it, to exploit it for individual or group advantage rather than to challenge it.

Finally, the very complexity and fragmentation of the Soviet multinational population enables the central leadership to exploit tensions and antagonisms to maintain control. For example, when Georgian elites were protesting constitutional changes that would affect the status of the Georgian language, the Abkhazian minority within Georgia appealed to Moscow for support in protecting their own national rights vis-a-vis the Georgians—a reminder of the limits of national self-assertion.

In conclusion, while there are conceivable circumstances under which various social forces, including national groups, could become increasingly politicized and could pose a serious threat to the stability of the Soviet system, such a prospect is highly unlikely in the near and medium term. Clearly, the political salience of national self-assertiveness is growing and is likely to impinge on the management of central problems, from the composition of the Central Committee and Politburo, to decisions about economic reform, to issues of foreign policy. The nationality problem creates complex challenges for the Soviet system and the new Soviet leadership, but it is unlikely to disrupt the stability of the Soviet system.

A WRITER MEETS THE STATE: LITERARY AUTHORSHIP IN MODERN RUSSIA

Alexander Rodchenko, "The Press is our Weapon," 1923

GREGORY FREIDIN

"The poet starts his tales from far away,
Tales take the poet far away...."
Marina Tsvetaeva

"Societies in which citizenship is a developing institution create an image of an ideal citizenship against which achievement can be measured and towards which aspirations can be directed."
T. H. Marshall

I want to sketch out the way modern Russian literature, in particular "engaged" literature, has been perceived in both Russia and the West in the post-Stalin decades. During this period, perhaps more noticeably than ever before, the production as well as the reception of Russian literature, including the nineteenth-century classics, has been shaped by the relation of literature to power. In fact, it would not be an exaggeration to say that most literary figures worth the name have invariably inserted themselves, their work, or the work of a reinterpreted earlier author into the political sphere. Whether it was to lend support to a particular undertaking by the government or—more notably if less frequently—to question the legitimacy of its actions or even its *raison d'être*, the role of the author in the evolution of the relationship between the governnment and the governed has been widely acknowledged. One need not go far to find examples of famous cases: the Pasternak affair (1958), the trial of the poet Joseph Brodsky for "social parasitism" (1964), the trials of Siniavsky and Daniel (1966), and, of course, the entire career of Alexander Solzhenitsyn. There is no denying that these and similar celebrated confrontations between the literati and the Soviet state have influenced the way an educated reader—American or Russian—has looked at Russian literature.

Indeed, these days we expect no less from a Russian author, who, for his part, was reared in the "heroic" tradition of literary authorship in Imperial Russia. The pithy dictum from Nekrasov's poem, "You need not be a poet, but a citizen—that you must be," rings over the literary terrain much as it did when it was issued in the middle of the nineteenth century. Then, as now, a call to citizenship in Russia had more to do with self-sacrifice in the cause of emancipation from despotism than with the legal framework for the exercise of "the rights of man." Molded in the image of this tradition, writers today must feel wary of disappointing their audience if they fail to live up to the old expectations that they themselves have helped to revive. Take this example:

> I divide all the works of world literature into the permitted ones and those written without permission. The first kind are junk, the second are stolen air. I want to spit in the face of the writers who write with an advance permission, I want to beat them on the head with a stick, I want them all seated at the Herzen House [Writers' Club] with a glass of police-man's tea in front of each. . . .
>
> I would make it illegal for these writers to get married and have children. How can they have children—after all, it is up to the children to continue our work, to tell to the end the most important part of our story—when the fathers have been sold to the pockmarked devil for the next three generations.

This admonition, which the poet Osip Mandelshtam flung at the writers' community in 1930, was in wide circulation among the literati in Moscow and Leningrad in the 1960s and 1970s. Its echoes can be heard in the legal and more decorous rhetoric of Solzhenitsyn's 1967 "Letter to the Fourth Congress of Soviet Writers":

> The right of our writers to voice judgements which are ahead of their time concerning the moral life of man and society, their right to an independent elucidation of social problems or of the historical experience of our country, *gained at the cost of such great suffering*—these rights are neither presupposed nor recognized. [Emphasis added]

However habitual they may be and perhaps, in fact, because they are habitual, these expectations of a writer's heroic stance do not make less puzzling the assumption that underlies them, namely, that literature, primarily Russian literature, is a source of genuine power and not just a political irritant, as some might suggest. To what extent, if at all, this assumption corresponds to the author's actual influence on the political process is another matter and one that warrants a separate discussion. For our purposes, I shall assume that public perception, especially as it involves the country's educated elite, is a force in its own right and, although hard to measure, should be counted among other, more generally acknowledged, societal forces.

In trying to understand the United States today, a discussion of the literary scene side by side with an analysis of "Star Wars" would be deemed out of place. That literature should rub shoulders with "real things" seems, however, almost inevitable when attention turns to Soviet Russia. Not everywhere is this seen to be the natural order of things. What, then, are the conditions that make possible the existence of this particular literary culture and how did they come about?

The first, and perhaps most important, condition of possibility is the *relative tolerance* of the present Soviet system. I emphasize both words for the simple reason that when either tolerance or intolerance comes close to being absolute—the United States today, and the Soviet Union in the late 1930s, 1940s, and the early 1950s, respectively—aesthetic institutions do not tend to encroach on the political sphere. It is another matter when repression is, as it has been in Russia since Stalin's death, only partial. Under circumstances like these a writer can take on the state even if the latter has at its disposal a formidable army and navy. How many divisions does Solzhenitsyn command? In more inclement political times, when politics were dominated by violence, this paraphrase of Stalin's dismissal of the Vatican's power could have been a fitting epitaph to the public ambitions of a Solzhenitsyn. But where violence is constrained, the calculus of a political strongman loses its applicability. In the history of Russian literature in the post-Stalin era, Solzhenitsyn is a prime example of the effect that the new limitations on violence have had on the cultural sphere, as well as a prime beneficiary of this development.

The second condition of possibility involves the association of a particular body of work with an unusual public personality, one capable of sustaining a charismatic aura in the eyes of the readership. In this respect, too, Solzhenitsyn offers a rewarding example. His

Gulag Archipelago helped to shape America's popular opinion of the Soviet Union—a matter not only of foreign policy but of internal United States politics as well. This four-volume *Essay in Literary Investigation*, as Solzhenitsyn subtitled his hybrid history of repression in the Soviet Union, had an even more dramatic effect on internal politics in France, where the Left has been an institutionalized part of government. The phenomenon of *The Gulag Archipelago* enabled the Socialist Party to increase its ranks, often at the expense of the French Communists. Remarkably, these developments were precipitated by a literary work, the story of its appearance, and, emphatically, the story of its author. The factual material contained in the volumes played only a secondary role, for the basic facts about Soviet repression, particularly under Stalin, had been well known and accessible to anyone in the West for decades.

What effect did Solzhenitsyn, as a literary personality, have in the Soviet Union, where he ought to have counted most? In the absence of public opinion polls or other avenues of free discussion, it is hard to measure or qualify his influence. Suffice it to say that Khrushchev's campaign of de-Stalinization, the single most important event in Russia since World War II, came to be identified as much with Solzhenitsyn and his novella, *One Day in the Life of Ivan Denisovich*, as with any one symbolic figure or phenomenon.

This uncanny capacity of the Russian literary culture to invest the author of fiction with the symbolic intensity of those historical events with which he has been associated largely as a passive agent, brings us to the third condition: that readers, including the government—indeed, above all the government—take literature seriously. They did so with Pasternak, Brodsky, Siniavsky, Daniel, Solzhenitsyn, and, more recently, with Voinovich and Aksyonov. The most celebrated example, the appearance of Solzhenitsyn's *The Gulag Archipelago*, had consequences powerful enough to warrant a full-scale press campaign of vilification against an author who had so recently been officially lionized.

Because he had been lavishly praised, he could not be easily silenced, and because in the eyes of the authorities literature mattered, he could not be ignored. The affair came to an end when the government decided to cut its political losses and to suffer an international embarrassment by expelling him—all in order to avoid the greater potential embarrassment of having to incarcerate him for a length of time. Or so it seemed then. In retrospect, it appears that damage ran much deeper but was obscured from sight by the anger many intellectuals felt toward the Soviet government for forcing into exile abroad Russia's foremost writer. But for the average Soviet citizen who remembered the good old days under Stalin, when as much as a peep landed you in jail for the rest of your life, a one-way ticket to the West, a coveted destination, signified a victory for the author and a defeat for the power of the state—the army and the navy notwithstanding.

Would it not have been more prudent for the authorities, we may reasonably inquire, to remain above the fray and to ignore Solzhenitsyn altogether? For they must have known that by engaging him even in this, by Soviet standards, gentle way, they were amplifying his voice and enhancing his stature, thereby sharing with the writer— a single individual—some of the world's greatest authority and might. This fellow Solzhenitsyn was worth a few divisions, after all. And let us not forget that well before the Solzhenitsyn affair and certainly since, more than a few authors have entered into a similar power-sharing arrangement with the Soviet state.

Apparently the government felt compelled to act as it did, and so did the author. In fact, the two parties were operating within a distinct tradition—a particular cultural arrangement, an anthropologist would call it—in which the author feels compelled to play the part of the lone bearer of truth, with the collective body of government filling the role of the other protagonist—the faceless, brawny, and humorless Goliath. This uneasy theatrical symbiosis not long ago prompted Andrei Siniavsky to show mock empathy for the pathetic Russian (including the Soviet) state:

> The time has come now to pity not the writers but their persecutors and oppressors, for it is to them that Russian literature owes its success. And what of the writer? He has no worries: there he is sitting calmly in prison or in the madhouse, hugging himself with delight: a story! And as he breathes his last, he can rub his hands: the job's done!

Needless to say, Siniavsky, who himself was launched on his public career as a writer of fiction by his arrest, trial, and subsequent lengthy imprisonment in the Gulag, had no intention of trivializing the personal tragedies of individual authors. But being a writer and a literary scholar, he could not avoid noting in the uncanny recurrence of this phenomenon a rewarding, almost archetypal dramatic plot. Thus literature's involvement with power has come full circle—from their earlier confrontations to their relationship as an accepted fact of social and political life, and, finally, to the ironic appreciation of the long-standing interdependence of literature and governmental repression.

There is special value in this dramatic, theatrical view of what Siniavsky called the "literary process in Russia." For it makes visible the background forces which, like the playwright, the producer, and the director in the real theater, define the outlines of the performance—to borrow a phrase from John LeCarré—in the theater of the real. In order to enter this stage, the authorities have to make everything, including literary production, their business; that is to say, they must maintain an absolute claim on power. But in order to remain on stage, they must accept limitations on what they can and cannot do, because the rules of theater, whether in politics or entertainment, require that even improvisation be coordinated with the invisible agencies behind the scenes. What is most paradoxical about a dramatic arrangement of this sort is that both the acceptance of limitations (implicit in a *political* process) and the unwillingness to share power with any one group (explicit in the authoritarian tradition of Russia, especially after 1917) must co-exist. Without this paradox, the famous show, "Writer Meets State," cannot go on.

Consider the alternatives: In the absence of this tacit deal, the stage, not to speak of the author, would be crushed under the weight of an unrestrained state power; if, on the other hand, the Soviet government were to acknowledge explicitly, as their modern counterparts have done, the legitimacy of autonomous non-governmental institutions, the production would have been cancelled even before the opening night. What, then, are the forces that maintain the precarious balance between the two asymmetrical protagonists on stage? Or, to pick up on the earlier question, how did this balance come about?

The answer lies in part in the modern Russian institution of authority, which, to resort to Max Weber's typology, blends the traditionalist view of the state as an immutable, almost patriarchal power (Father-Tsar or Father-Stalin) with the rational bureaucratic system that befits a modern industrial nation, and then combines the two with a very strong propensity for bringing forth intensely charismatic figures. Whereas no society can claim to be based on a single pure type of authority (the types are analytical abstractions), in a modern Western state, the universalist, legal-bureaucratic (that is, rational and predictable) type of authority is assumed to predominate overall. The kind of citizenship that emerges in such a society, too, is based on a universalist rationality. It may be said that the legal-rational state and the concept of citizenship represent two sides of the same coin and, indeed, they have historically developed together.

Russia offers a far more complex case. There the apparatus of rational authority did not evolve out of the indigenous institutions, as it had in the West, but has had to exist in parallel with them and absorb some of their qualities. Hence, in terms of Weber's typology, the power of the Russian state has been more traditionalist-autocratic (under the tsars) or dictatorial (under the Bolsheviks) and, especially in this century with its massive dislocations and instability, tended to concentrate in the hands of charismatic leaders (Lenin, Trotsky, Stalin). The concept as well as the institution of citizenship that has evolved under these circumstances bears the contradictory traits of both universality—for it is a set of rational principles—*and* radical exclusivity, because, for the most part, these principles have applied to and benefited only the country's elite.

It is among this latter—and in proportion to the population, relatively small—class that writers form a particularly privileged group. Especially in the Soviet period, with its truly draconian censorship, writers have turned out to be the only ones who can use the modern means of communication, whatever the limitations, for individual expression. In this regard, they even preempt the Party itself, which holds a monopoly on the media. After all, no Party official, with the exception of the supreme leader, can address the public in his, or her, own name but only in the name of the Party. This is one of the most significant although frequently ignored reasons why authorship and citizenship in Russia have become intimately intertwined. The field of individual expression, for historical reasons virtually the sole province of fine letters in Russia, has come to define citizenship: that imaginary but socially and politically palpable space where the power of the state encounters the fullest complement of the citizen's rights and powers implied in the notion of a "modern rational State."

When the government prevents an author from publishing his work—through censorship or, more benignly, by the use of its monopoly on public dissemination—or when the government confiscates the manuscript or, worst of all, when it arrests an author ostensibly for what he has written, our verdict is that the author's civil rights have been violated. But the same is true sooner or later for every Soviet citizen. Still, the writers' case is special. Unlike other citizens, they can practice their *profession*—including not only *individual* expression but also a *mass-scale* dissemination—only to the extent that their rights as citizens of a modern state are not circumscribed. In this respect, a professional Russian author becomes a professional citizen. The answer will be the same if we see an author prevented by the government from participating in the political process. Only now what is violated is the author's political rights—once again, his rights as a citizen.

These are the terms—civil and political rights of citizens—that constitute the basis of our thought on the travails of the Russian author. And in Russia, too, many appeals on behalf of writers and artists have been made by invoking the Soviet Constitution, which supposedly guarantees these rights, albeit with the proviso that they must not conflict with the leading role of the Party in the society and the state. To a legal scholar, this condition may represent an insoluble quandary, but a literary historian accepts this paradox wholeheartedly, accustomed as he is to poetic license and wishful thinking. We do not dispute the poet when he calls somebody, say, eternally young. He himself knows that it cannot be and we know that it cannot be, but we still like to hear it and he to sing about it. In a similar way, no matter how devastating its consequences, this spoil-sport condition in the constitution of the USSR is compelled to share the limelight with the sweet music of the universal rights of citizenship. And because they belong to the modern institution of literary authorship, the writers are obliged, as it were, to walk on both sides of the street, provided they wish to continue practicing their profession.

There are, of course, other reasons for singling out the writers as a group. While these days writers are far from being the only group insisting on their rights—national and religious groups are, in fact, in the forefront—in the post-Stalin years, both the primacy and visibility belonged to the writers of fiction and poetry. And I would insist that our concern with Soviet citizenship is still focused primarily on writers. A Russian writer, then, is not merely a citizen; he is that, of course, but he is primarily a sort of symbolic citizen —in his own eyes as well as those of his public at home and abroad.

Finally, for a variety of reasons, Russian authors are more likely than their Western counterparts to generate an intense charismatic aura. However "modern" their profession, its imperatives, such as individuality and insistence on unrestricted access to the public, tend to be interpreted in the light of the far more archaic, indigenous institutions of itinerant sages and holy men. Here many different strains of Russian culture, some new, some as old as Byzantium, converge and conjoin. The modern rights of citizenship and mass communications begin to blend with the holy man's invocation of a divine calling. Preoccupation with ethical and spiritual questions, which have no other public forum in Russia except literature, becomes inseparable from prophecy or spiritual enlightenment. Modern individualism of literary expression recalls the individuality of sainthood, and the victimization of the author by such a modern "rational" institution as political police repression comes to be identified with the tradition of martyrdom. The story of Solzhenitsyn is, once again, instructive in this regard. And those who have seen Samuel Rachlin's television documentary about the Soviet singer, poet, and actor Vladimir Vysotsky can now visualize how the modern *popularity* of a verbal artist (based on the medium of magnetic tape) can, in the instant of an artist's death, be converted into a public demonstration with political overtones and the intensity of a virtual religious cult.

It is worth noting, in conclusion, that the popular "sanctification" of Vysotsky happened despite the fact that he had not been persecuted by the authorities—he had in fact enjoyed a modicum of official recognition and died of complications associated with a predilection for strong drink. This was, then, a rare occasion when a writer met the state halfway, although the state, perhaps enlightened by Siniavsky's ironic observation, did not seem to be willing to keep to the letter of the old script. For their part, the audience, who had memorized it through decades of repetition, seemed unaware of the change. It will take more than one improvisation to break the spell of one of Russia's longest running shows.

DISSENT IN THE SOVIET UNION

Poster from Hoover Institution Archives collection, artist unknown

ROBERT CONQUEST

Dissent in the Soviet Union must be seen in the perspectives both of history and of current world politics; but it is, in its present form, a fairly new phenomenon. "Dissent" is a good and descriptive word; it implies that there is a dominant and pervasive orthodoxy, and that the dissenters are those who claim the right to think for themselves, to seek the truth directly, and to say or write that the positions of Soviet orthodoxy are based largely on established untruth. The earliest output of dissent in the late 1950s and early 1960s consisted to a great extent of attempts to recover and circulate the facts of Soviet history. Because these efforts were denied or suppressed, they inevitably led to a struggle for civil rights, and in particular for freedom of expression.

We should not, however, think in terms of nothing existing but pure dogma and pure dissent. There has been a gray area in between, varying in scope from year to year, where fiction writers in particular have been allowed to publish material implying, or even openly suggesting, some unorthodox point. In the early 1980s, for example, several writers described the man-made famine of 1933, which is officially still non-existent. Although significant in its way, however, this border zone is fairly narrow and has far less impact than dissent proper.

We may judge the extent of that impact if we consider the great names in Soviet culture and note how many of them are either in exile abroad or under persecution at home—in both cases for wishing to express ideas or recount facts unacceptable to the Soviet leadership. Writers, scientists, musicians—the cream of the country, they are headed by the two colossal figures of Andrei Sakharov and Aleksander Solzhenitsyn.

To speak these two names is to bring to our minds the fact that the dissidents, though all reject Soviet orthodoxy, hold differing views. Except for a few extraordinary fringe elements like the bizarre groups of young Nazis and Maoists, we find the main body including such men (even if as an exception) as Roy Medvedev, who considers himself a Leninist and hopes for improvement through the Party. His dissidence consists mainly of telling the truth about Stalinism and urging a certain extension of liberty within the Leninist state. Most of the dissidents regard this as a chimera, but it is worth noting as a possible element in any future evolution of the Soviet regime to something in the nature of the USSR in the Khrushchev period, when the political climate resembled the cold of Greenland, rather than the extreme frigidity of Antarctica, as it does at present.

The bulk of the dissidence may be divided, very roughly, between the two main tendencies exemplified by Sakharov and Solzhenitsyn. Sakharov is the model of the type often characterized as "liberal"— one who hopes for a Western style future for Russia—while Solzhenitsyn is taken to typify a Russian traditionalist view, which foresees a period of evolution, with the regime or its successor first becoming a limited autocracy. It is certainly true that the tone of Sakharov is different from that of Solzhenitsyn. On the one hand you have an internationalist democrat, and on the other a religious traditionalist. Solzhenitsyn is often called a "nationalist," and so he is in the sense that he sees the Russian nation as a special case whose sufferings enable it to make a particular contribution to the world. (But he and those like him do not favor Russian expansionism.) For his part, Sakharov does not see democracy coming immediately; he also thinks of a transitional period. And he, too, looks back on the civic progress made before the Revolution as most valuable, thus in a way sharing Solzhenitsyn's attitude toward the past. In spite of their differences, which are important, the views of both fall within the general aim of human dignity.

These are the two main currents. But we have so far spoken only of Russian dissidents centered in Moscow. There are also, among the Jews, Zionists who wish to emigrate to Israel. Other Jews simply wish to join their relatives in the West and apply for passports, upon which they lose their jobs—at a minimum—and live in a sort of purgatory as "refuseniks." In the great majority of cases they are not allowed out, although a few are permitted to leave—sometimes after years. Also, there are the dissidents of the non-Russian republics of the USSR. And in many of these areas the numbers are much greater and the extent of sympathy, even in Party circles, broader than is the case in Moscow. This is especially true of the Baltic States, the Ukraine, Georgia, the North Caucasus, and other areas.

We have not yet mentioned the religious dissidents—not the religious philosophers, like some of the Solzhenitsyn circle, but the membership of actual churches, such as the illegal Baptists, who will not accept the leaders imposed on the "official" Baptists by the authorities. The Baptists in labor camps probably outnumber any other dissident category. Other illegal religions include the Jehovah's Witnesses—who will compromise with no government—and the Ukrainian Catholics of the Eastern Rite, whose church was forcibly annexed to the Russian Orthodox Church in 1945 but still exists in the underground, with illegal publications, an illegal priesthood, and even (at least until quite recently) an underground nunnery. They too are strongly represented in the labor camps, although usually in their role of Ukrainian nationalists.

What are the numbers of the dissidents? This cannot be easily determined. In Khrushchev's time the then head of the secret police, Semichastny, is reported as saying that if he were allowed to arrest 2,000 people, the Moscow dissidents would be finished. Perhaps he underestimated—and, of course, his figure does not take into account those outside the capital. At any rate, there are many more than this, as we shall see, at present in labor camps on political charges, while dissidents are also often sentenced on non-political pretexts, such as being "parasites."

How far beyond the active dissidents does sympathy with their ideas penetrate? There are people who are not precisely dissidents and yet not precisely "right" from the official point of view. The only numerical test I have ever come upon was about six or seven years ago, when a school teacher was fired from her job because she had stood outside the court at one of the trials in which dissidents were being sentenced. Of the fifty-odd teachers who voted, five voted not to fire her and another ten abstained, which means that more than a quarter of this particular school in Moscow (which certainly may not be typical) did show reluctance to follow the line at least on one point. That possibly indicates what the potential may be among the intelligentsia of that type. As for the wider public, one recent poll is reported as showing that about 20 percent of the population sympathized with Sakharov. In some of the republics—the Baltic States in particular—dissidence is extremely widespread. Several hundred thousand signatures were collected for a single petition of complaint, for example—an astonishingly large number in Soviet circumstances. Indeed, all the indications we have show that the Baltic populations (whose incorporation into the USSR is not recognized by the West) yearn for independence.

In Central Asia there is some dispute about how far nationalism and Islam, represented in the "Mohammedan Brotherhoods" constitute trouble, but in the North Caucasus they certainly do. This is a much smaller area than Central Asia, with a population of only a few million. Soviet accounts describing the Brotherhoods there as illegal have reported that they have 200,000 members—again, a huge figure under Soviet conditions. This anti-Soviet feeling derives in part from the fact that these are the nations that were deported from their homelands under Stalin, with the consequent death of about one-third of their members (those who survived were allowed to return under Khrushchev except in the case of two nations which remain in exile). It is very difficult for the KGB (Secret Police) to penetrate these Brotherhoods, because they are based on the clan system that still persists in these areas.

An important point to make about the active dissidents is that their methods are, normally, completely legal under Soviet law. *Samizdat*, "self-publication," consists of typing out six copies of something on the typewriter. This is not illegal. It is illegal to have Xeroxes or printing machines for such a purpose. But, of course, anyone writing a book that has not yet been censored is entitled to make his own one or two copies; the act itself is not illegal, and the dissident can be charged only on the basis of the content of his piece—when and if it falls into police hands.

Similarly, demonstrations as such are not illegal. Indeed, the right to demonstrate is guaranteed under the Soviet constitution. And

when dissidents demonstrate, they usually stand around and do nothing or at most raise a banner saying, "Observe the Constitution." For a time, this to some small degree baffled the authorities, and demonstrators were attacked by thugs, arrested for a few hours, warned and released. Nowadays such demonstrations are very rare and are ruthlessly suppressed. Some government acts, like the exiling of Sakharov, have no basis whatever in Soviet law. But, in addition to such illegality, the rulers still operate a complex and rather pettifogging attempt at legalism and "trials." There was an Estonian trial a year or two ago, which was reported in the press—unfortunately, before it had taken place—with all of its results and sentences. The authorities hadn't told the paper it had been postponed, but it got the sentences right just the same.

Nowadays the dissidents are not, generally speaking, tortured, as they would, of course, have been in Stalin's time. This does not apply to common criminals, who are often beaten up—in Georgia, reportedly until a few years ago under the aegis of the new Soviet Foreign Minister, Shevardnadze, who was then the Georgian Police Minister. What is done instead to the "politicals" is to place them in KGB psychiatric hospitals. (There were three of these when Andropov took over; he raised them to about thirty in number.) There they can legally apply to prisoners painful, demoralizing, and non-curative torture drugs, together with various unpleasant methods of "restraint."

Dissidents are also, and more commonly, sent to labor camps. The ration scale is about the same as in Stalin's time, which is rather less than the prisoners were given in the camps on the River Kwai by the Japanese. But it is possible, usually, to survive. To see someone like Sinyavsky, the art critic, is extraordinary: a tiny little man who did seven years for writing a couple of books. You wouldn't have thought he would have survived a week. There is a great toughness in some of these people. Many do die through lack of medical treatment and from improper diet; several such deaths are reported almost every week.

Meanwhile, outside the camps, there is general harassment as well as beatings in the streets by unknown people. Exiles not officially jailed live in odd corners of Siberia under heavy pressures. By such measures, year after year, the authorities have broken a few individual dissidents down to the degree that they appear on television and retract their views.

Over the last few years, and especially in the last few months, the dissidents have been treated more and more harshly. They would be in even worse condition, they all insist, but for the existence of Western public opinion. But now, for example, the Helsinki monitoring groups, to which most of the more important active dissidents in Moscow, Georgia, Kiev, and other parts of the USSR belong, has been very much whittled down. Of its fifteen leading Moscow activists, only two remain at liberty, unable to act. The other groups are in even worse condition: The present regime seems to have taken a decision to crush them.

The above is a very rough run-through of what the dissidents face and what they try to do. Perhaps more important is what drives them—I suggest, above all, the urges to liberty and to truth. I have known Soviet historians who became very active simply because they couldn't stand reading the textbooks. In looking at a brand new (1984) *Encyclopedia of the Civil War* I note that there is no entry on Trotsky, who commanded the Red Army. (There is an entry on Trotskyism, but it merely says how wrong Trotskyism was in various Party debates of the time, mainly on trade unions.) Unless you live in that atmosphere of falsification and suppression, I do not think you can envisage how infuriating it must be to know you are expected to be fooled. Fake photographs, of course, are a tradition in the Soviet Union, right back to the famous one in which Stalin and Kamenev were photographed in exile together, in the later versions of which we see Stalin and a small tree in Kamenev's place. There are dozens of such instances. They persist to the present day. Two recent examples involve cosmonauts. In each case two versions of a photo were available through some slip-up, and in each case one cosmonaut has disappeared—one has merged into a door pillar and the other, in an airplane, has become a window. That is a direct insult to the intelligence of any student or anyone else who happens to come across it.

To return to encyclopedias: On occasion you have to remove pages from them and put in new ones. Again, I was surprised recently to find that the 1939 census is still regarded as valid, even though it is known to have been faked. In fact, in Khrushchev's time they more or less rehabilitated—rather quietly—the genuine 1937 census, which had been suppressed and the census board shot for "diminishing the population of the Soviet Union." Well, if you are a demographer it must be annoying to see this treated seriously. The great terror famine of 1932–1933, in which millions died, was occasionally referred to in fiction of the early 1980s; control was laxer in fiction than in textbooks, in which it is not mentioned at at all. Omission as well as straight falsification is practiced. Nowadays there is no account at all, pro or con, of the great political events of 1936–1938, the Moscow Trials in which most of Lenin's colleagues confessed to being traitors and were shot. Stalin had his story that they were traitors and should be shot, and we had our version—long since proved true—that it was all a big frame-up. But the present regime simply avoids the subject.

Of course, Soviet life consists of more than the reading of history, which brings us to what one writer calls "the stifling air of deceit" in every sphere. The Constitution, which guarantees freedom of practically everything, is in itself a fake in that sense. And elections: Their word for election, *vybor*, means the same as ours, "choice"; but they have only one name on the ballot. At the level of ordinary life we may note a book, *Galina*, by Galina Vishnevskaya, the great soprano, who is now in the West with her husband, Mstislav Rostropovich. An astonishing book, it gives a number of examples of the shameless falsifications that she met with. One story she tells is of La Scala's coming to Moscow from Milan. A representative of the company went round to the Ministry of Culture to tell them that La Scala would like Galina to sing *Tosca* with them. The answer was that Galina didn't sing *Tosca*. When the Italian protested that she had sung in a La Scala performance of the opera the year before, the culture official replied that Galina was not in Moscow. On learning from the La Scala representative that indeed she was in Moscow and was as a matter of fact dining with him that very evening, the official dismissed him with a promise to call him in half an hour and give him a final answer. The final answer was that Galina refused to sing *Tosca*. When the La Scala man went round to dinner with her and asked if she had really refused to sing it, she answered that of course it was untrue. Upon his expressing astonishment, she explained, "You're in the Soviet Union." And that is but one of several similar stories she recounts.

Another book, *The Ivankiad*, by Vladimir Voinovich, gives a feel for the Soviet Union and for Soviet life in connection with officialdom in a small way—nothing terrible, just petty nastiness. It is simply an account of how Sergey Ivanko, a prominent literary bureaucrat who had not himself written anything much, tried to stop the author from getting a suitable flat at the Writers' Union block for his family, because

"I KNOW IT WORKED WITH THE DISSIDENTS, COMRADE ANDROPOV—
BUT I DON'T THINK WE CAN EXILE THE <u>ECONOMY</u>...."

he, Ivanko, wanted to enlarge his own already illegally large flat. A story of intrigue and lies, it ends with a letter from the granddaughter of the great Russian writer Chukovsky saying how the same Ivanko, as head of a publishing enterprise, had for some time prevented the publication of her grandfather's collection of autographed stories, memoirs, and bits and pieces by all the great writers, singers, and other luminaries of Russia. Ivanko explained to her, "It can't be printed now, the roof of the printing house has fallen in and smashed all the plates." So she rushed around to the printing house and found a strong concrete building that had never experienced any such accident. Ivanko, however, held the book up for years; when it eventually emerged, it emerged cut. Ivanko is at present an enthusiastic media spokesman for the new clean government.

I have not dealt with, or only barely, one phenomenon related to dissent, and that is the Russian national movement found among certain fiction writers and others. This is a fairly new phenomenon, and it is worth special attention because over the past few years the Party has been trying to decide whether to use this Russian national feeling in its own interests. These nationalists are concerned mainly with the roots of Russia, the ancient villages, the ancient icons. If we leave aside some special, slightly far-out fantasies in which some of the rich young in Moscow have icons of the tsar and celebrate the White Armies, the movement is basically an attempt to preserve and use Russian national feeling—not in any virulent sense.

We can get some idea of the extent of this feeling from the huge attendance at two exhibitions of idealized pictures of the Russian past, in Leningrad and Moscow. Over a million and a half people went to them, and the comments in the visitor books (now available in the West) show vast support, not just from literary intellectuals, but from engineers, bureaucrats, the whole range of urban Russia. Five or six years ago, writers were producing stories about the Russian past, and indeed even implying that collectivization of the land had destroyed the Russian soul. A crackdown on these came in 1982, and in the last two or three years there has been a struggle by some in the literary bureaucracy to persuade these Russian writers to go on being Russian but to give up being liberal. Perhaps the Party's tactics will succeed, at least up to a point. But this large group of people, concerned with preserving the Russian past, overlaps with the totally anti-Soviet Russian nationalism of Solzhenitsyn.

I would like to end with the matter of the Helsinki Agreement. The aim of the Helsinki monitoring group is to see how the Soviet Union is observing the provisions of that agreement, signed ten years ago, and in particular the so-called "Basket Three," its human rights section. We are often told that no one really expects Moscow to observe human rights because their definition of human rights is so different from our own. But this does not apply to Helsinki, because it lays down quite clearly and factually what the signatory states expected—that is, the free movement of people and ideas. And it is not utopian; it speaks only of an increase in, and improvements in, the free movement of people and ideas. This of course has not taken place in the USSR, although its signature "solemnly binds" the Soviet government. There is a view in the West, and indeed among strong supporters of the dissidents, that the whole Helsinki Agreement should be abrogated on the grounds that the Soviet Union has failed to observe Basket Three—the other sections of the agreement being to the advantage of the Soviet Union.

My view and that of some of the dissidents is the opposite. The human rights issues were brought into the Helsinki treaty at the insistence of some of the smaller European powers, not on grounds of human rights as such, but on grounds of promoting peace. And this is how the Helsinki monitoring groups see them. Peaceful relations between states in the long run are not compatible with a condition of ideological siege on either side. We are not asking the Soviet Union to do this in order to be nice, but in order to improve the prospects of peace. This is the line taken by Sakharov, and by others in the movement—that they regard the lack of human rights we are speaking of as deleterious to peace. We can, I think, look at it in a similar sense: What they do to the dissidents—who are mainly democrats, Christians, whatever—is, one presumes, what they could do to any democrats, Christians, whatever, that they could lay their hands on, including, given the chance, us. I can leave you with that thought, that the dissidents are really just us in another geographical area.

CIVIL-MILITARY RELATIONS IN THE MID-1980S

V. Lebedev, "Setting to Work, Keep Your Rifle at Hand," *1921*

TIMOTHY J. COLTON

t is difficult to conceive of the Soviet regime without its military establishment. The two often seem to go together in our perception of the USSR—and that is not a mere figment of the Western imagination. The association is the product of Soviet history, and it is one the regime itself is quite happy to own up to. The Kremlin is not one bit embarrassed to be identified with military power. It is proud of Soviet military prowess and wastes few opportunities to convey this to its own population and to the rest of the world.

The Soviet Army, or Red Army as it was called in those days, was founded in the spring of 1918, only a few months after the genesis of the Soviet regime in the Bolshevik Revolution of 1917. The army grew side by side, indeed hand in hand, with the Soviet state and the Communist Party. In the early years, the army played a vital role in enabling the regime to quell its enemies in the long and bloody Russian civil war. A decade or a decade and a half later, Joseph Stalin gave the armed forces a prominent place in the politics, economics, and culture of the mature Soviet system. You could not look at Stalin's Russia, or at the life of an ordinary person in it, without being aware of the military fact.

Stalin's army, of course, suffered terribly, as did every other institution, from his crimes, suspicion, and, at times, arbitrary decisions.

Many officers fell victim to secret police terror in the late 1930s and then in several lesser waves after the war. On the other hand, those in military positions fortunate enough to escape the purges also benefited tremendously from Stalin's system. His program of economic and social modernization placed great emphasis on the development of military strength. Officers were, by the standards of the day, well paid and well housed. Between 1941 and 1945, the army was central to the Soviet effort in the "Great Patriotic War" against Hitler, a struggle which even today gets a place in official ideology and myth second only to the Revolution. Its top commanders were national heroes.

When Stalin died in 1953, his successors inherited a potent military machine, which they have since maintained and updated at considerable cost. At times they have quarreled with the military establishment, but they have never ignored it. Nor should we.

It would be difficult to overlook the military even if we wanted to. It is, to begin with, a very large and visible organization. The numbers here are subject to some dispute, as are most statistics bearing on the Soviet Union, but an estimate of 5 million men under arms would not be far off. That is about 5 percent of the male population. The military lays claim, and here again the numbers are not beyond controversy, to roughly 15 percent of the Soviet Gross National Product, about double the share of military spending in the American economy.

The Soviet military enterprise is administered by a bureaucracy of epic porportions. The Soviets take the normal stuff of military bureaucracy—size, specialization, immersion in routines and rituals—and stretch it to an extreme.

Any single-party regime is sure to be concerned with the behavior of its army, for in theory the latter is better situated than any other group to usurp the party's power. When the military is as expensive and as capable as the Soviet Army, it is doubly certain that civil-military relations will be taken seriously by the regime.

How do we begin thinking about this subject? The Soviets usually start their own discussions of specific problems with a formula of some kind. In this instance, the formula is disarmingly simple: the so-called "principle of Party leadership of the armed forces." This dictum might not tell us a lot if we tried to apply it uncritically to another communist regime, such as Poland or Cuba or China, where institutions are aligned differently. In the Soviet case, however, it is quite informative.

Put simply, the Soviets believe in civilian supremacy over military personnel and in the resolution of military problems. In the final analysis, Gorbachev and his colleagues in the Politburo have the final say on military decisions. They are also responsible for identifying, mobilizing, and managing the resources outside the military establishment—particularly the economic resources—that are needed to make good on the country's military commitments. The civilian bosses possess a number of tested instruments for checking their military subordinates. They have a well-articulated system for educating and indoctrinating military personnel, mostly enlisted men but also career officers. They have an efficient system for controlling appointments and career progression in the officer corps. They have in the KGB (Secret Police) an armed force of their own ready to be used against military dissenters or coup-makers.

It would be a mistake, however, to give undue emphasis to conflicts, actual and potential, between the Soviet Army and the Communist Party. When all is said and done, the two organizations have gotten along quite well over the years. In structural terms, there is a great deal of overlap between them. Party and army are separate for certain purposes but very much intertwined for others. More than 90 percent of all Soviet military commanders belong to the Communist Party, and most of the rest are members of the Party Youth League. In fact, no young man in the Soviet Union would dream of embarking on a military career without planning on eventually joining the Party as well.

The Party, for its part, has been receptive, particularly in recent decades, to decision input from its military instrument. Far from being determined to silence the military, it has gone to some lengths to see to it that it gets the advice it thinks it needs from the General Staff and other military agencies. On many issues of national security, it has made it difficult if not impossible for non-military officials to weigh in. More than that, the uniformed military is also well represented within the Party's own decision-making structure. The Central Committee of the Party, which is made up of the top 300 or so Soviet officials and meets in Moscow several times a year, contains several dozen generals and admirals. The same is true at the regional and local level. It is as if, in American terms, you had the military brass sitting in the Senate, the House of Representatives, the California State Legislature, and the San Francisco Board of Supervisors.

When it comes to attitudes and styles, a similar degree of cooperation can be found. Both Party and army, if one can generalize, celebrate hierarchy and discipline. Both are intensely nationalistic and are dominated by ethnic Russians. Both have tended to see life, politics included, as first and foremost an exercise in combat. They share an insecurity toward the outside world that is perhaps changing in form but seems not to be changing very much in essence.

If we had the leisure to comb through the Soviet historical record in detail, we would find many unexplained episodes in civil-military relations, and some for which Western scholars and analysts offer conflicting interpretations. But there would be near unanimity on one thing: that during the Brezhnev period, that is from the mid-1960s to the early 1980s, relations between civilian and military leaders were unusually good. We may some day in hindsight have to modify this picture, but for the moment we are safe in saying that the Brezhnev era was one of relative stability and harmony in Party-army relations.

This is in part explained by the conservative style of the Brezhnev Politburo, which revered many of the things that military officers instinctively respect. The leadership's nostalgia, and especially its veneration of the Soviet Union's experience and sacrifices in the war, were, for obvious reasons, viewed with favor by many Soviet officers. Brezhnev and his colleagues were much inclined to leave veteran officials in all spheres in place, and the senior military, in particular, found this congenial. The leadership also tended to defer to professionals and specialists in making decisions, and it did not treat the military in that respect much differently from other Soviet elites.

Personalities also contributed to civil-military amity. The most important was undoubtedly Brezhnev himself, who earlier in his career had had great exposure to military life. He had been a Party commissar in the army on several occasions and rose to a general's rank in the war. In the latter half of the 1950s, he had supervised military industry and the space program as Nikita Khrushchev's right-hand man in that area. He was consequently well versed in military affairs and had numerous connections with senior officers.

The other individual who deserves mention is the late Minister of Defense, Dmitri Ustinov. Ustinov became minister in 1976, when some of the difficulties we will examine were beginning to become evident. A civilian administrator, he had been the most powerful figure in defense industry for the previous thirty-five years, in the course of which he had become well acquainted with Brezhnev. Ustinov had a perhaps unique credibility with both the military and the

Party leadership, and until his death in December 1984 he was probably an effective balance wheel between the two.

Having outlined the background to the present situation, let us now turn to changes in the environment of civil-military relations. It is easier to point to these changes than to demonstrate a clear response on the part of civilian and military leaders. At a minimum, we can say that some of the preconditions for a modification of the Party-army relationship are in place.

Let us first look at the environmental change in the political arena, where several trends, at times contradictory, can be detected. The Soviet Union, as we all know, is in the throes of a major transformation of its leadership. The advanced years and increasingly infirm health of the country's top politicians were increasingly evident from the mid-1970s on. In the early 1980s, one infirm General Secretary was succeeded by another. There was talk in the Western media of a power vacuum in Moscow. The lack of strong direction at the very heart of the regime seemed to many observers to leave more room for other actors, the military included, to assert themselves.

This transition was bound to reach some kind of resolution, and it is now doing so at a brisk pace. The Brezhnev generation is now disappearing from the Soviet elite. Merely to list the members of the old guard dead or retired since 1980 is to make the point: Brezhnev, Kosygin, Suslov, Kirilenko, Pel'she, Andropov, Chernenko, Romanov, Tikhonov. The winners in the struggle to succeed them—Mikhail Gorbachev and the others—have been not only individually but also collectively a newer and much younger generation of officials. The new leaders, without in any way resolving the underlying problems of the Soviet system, have at least opened up to greater scrutiny and debate the question of the long-term priorities, and perhaps even the ultimate structure and shape, of the Soviet regime.

Generational change has also been proceeding within the military establishment. Ustinov's successor as defense minister, Marshal Sergei Sokolov, is an interim appointee, a man in his seventies apparently preferred by the then general secretary, Konstantin Chernenko, to younger alternatives. At lower levels, however, we are seeing new faces coming to the fore, men who are anywhere from five to twenty years younger than the veterans they are replacing. Six officers who have been promoted since 1980 to the position of commander of a military district or its equivalent were born in 1930 or later. For example, the new commander of the Transcaucasus Military District, General Arkhipov, was born in 1933, making him two years younger than Gorbachev; the new commander of Soviet troops in Hungary, General Kochetov, was born in 1932. Six other newcomers at this level were born in 1928 or 1929. These are not exactly raw recruits, but they are mid-career professionals who have acquired their general's stars relatively recently.

There has been a great deal of discussion in the West about the meaning of the generational change within the Soviet civilian elite. As far as the military leadership is concerned, we have far less hard evidence to go on, but there is reason to believe that the younger men are going to be different in certain ways. They are, one suspects, going to be more impatient with Soviet shortcomings than the older men they are supplanting and more open to policy innovation within the overall framework of the Soviet political order.

A second major area of change and potential impact on the civil-military balance is the Soviet economy. Let us take it as established that the Soviets have experienced a distressing slowdown in growth that, for a variety of reasons, accelerated in the late 1970s and has had serious effects throughout the Soviet system. Not the least of these effects has been a squeeze on the military budget. The precise nature of this squeeze is a matter of some debate in the West. The majority view among analysts who have access to the classified data necessary to a thorough study of the question is that the rate of increase of Soviet military spending was halved after 1976, from an annual increase after inflation of 4 or 5 percent over the previous decade to something like 2 percent since then. Other Western experts see it differently, acknowledging that the rate of deployment of expensive weapon systems has decelerated since 1976 but explaining this in terms of greater goldbricking and an increased taste for optimal design within the Soviet research and development system.

Either way, the news is bad for the Soviet military. Censorship prevents most Soviet officers from openly discussing how the budget crunch has affected military hardware. But the message comes through loud and clear in Soviet military publications, which now carry more insistent demands than at any time in recent memory for conservation of fuel and other resources within the military establishment. There is evidence that because of the string of poor harvests in the last few years greater pressure has been brought to bear on the Soviet military units to grow their own food. One also finds more frequent and angrier articles about things like line-ups, shortages of consumer goods, and petty corruption among sales personnel within the Ministry of Defense, all of which irritate the military officer no less than his counterpart out of uniform.

There can be little doubt that the sag in growth rates has led to fiercer competition within the Soviet system—part of it open, part of it submerged—over economic resources. One can infer from the substance and tone of public statements that some Soviet military leaders believe that they deserve more generous allocation of resources than they have been getting. There are clearly some civilians, particularly in the consumer sector and in the provincial apparatus of the Party, who feel the military's resource bite more acutely than they did ten or fifteen years ago and would prefer to see the military's share reduced.

A third and related area of substantial change, which may contribute to civil-military tension in post-Brezhnev Soviet politics, is that of military technology. For good reason, the Soviets have been increasingly convinced of the dynamism of military technology and concerned about the difficulty of keeping up with their arch-adversary, the United States. In fact, Leonid Brezhnev, in his next to last public appearance in October 1982, felt called upon to address the entire assembled military high command on this subject. He was motivated, we have to assume, by the pace of the Reagan rearmament program and by Israel's great success against Syrian-manned Soviet weapons in the June 1982 fighting in Lebanon. His message was clear: The struggle for supremacy in military technology had "sharply accelerated" and was taking on "a fundamentally new character." The Soviet Union could not dare fall behind.

The Soviets have for some time now spoken of a "revolution in military affairs," by which they have meant largely the changes connected with the introduction of nuclear weapons. They now show an increasing tendency to define this revolution more broadly, to pay more attention to conventional weaponry, and to give particular emphasis to microelectronics and communications technology, which some argue may in the end have as many implications for warfare as nuclear arms. President Reagan's Strategic Defense Initiative, unveiled five months after Brezhnev's death, has driven home the point that the USSR's lag in technological innovation may put it at a competitive disadvantage that will be difficult to offset through the traditional quantitative means.

Recent developments also seem to have provoked some rethinking in Moscow on the connection between military and civilian technology. Soviet planners, who in the past have regarded innovation in military technology as something best promoted in highly specialized, usually secrecy-enshrouded institutes insulated from the civilian sector, now must confront the fact that so many of the recent breakthroughs in Western practice have come about in exactly the opposite way. If dynamism in military technology depends in the late twentieth century on a healthy and progressive civilian economy, then Soviet strategists necessarily must become more interested in larger questions of economic management and reform—and there is some evidence that this is one path they have been following.

Another dimension of the environment of civil-military relations in which changes have been occurring is the social dimension. Pick any negative trend in Soviet society that you like—alcohol abuse, ethnic friction, decline in public morale, problems in the health care system—and you can find that trend echoed and represented within the Soviet military establishment. The regiment commander or general staff officer does not have to read in *Pravda* (let alone the *New York Times*) about these things. He can see them with his own eyes in the barracks or on the drill ground. More research would have to be done to establish how deeply officers' perceptions of their own society have been affected by their experience of social malaise among their recruits and civilian contacts, but there is enough on the public record to suggest a greater awareness, at least on the part of the Soviet military, of unfavorable trends in Soviet life.

A final area in which potentially unsettling change can be detected is the international environment. The deterioration in Soviet-American relations has led many in the Soviet military to view with growing alarm the military and strategic interaction with the United States. Soviet officers also see increasing strain, which directly involves the Soviet military, in the Third World. Prior to 1970, Soviet involvements here were very limited. Today the USSR is fighting a war in Afghanistan, a small war by European standards, but a war nonetheless. The Soviet military is also involved far more than it was a generation ago in military assistance missions and arms transfer arrangements, all of which bring greater interaction with Party, Foreign Ministry, and KGB officials who share policy responsibilities in this area.

A development abroad that has evoked concern within the Soviet military, and in a different way within the Party, is the altered situation in Poland, the USSR's most important military ally. Here is a neighbor, a member of the Warsaw Pact, governed by a Leninist party—but in which, since 1981, a uniformed army general has been head of both the government and the ruling party. The Polish crisis does not seem to have had immediate effects on Soviet military politics. But it has to have served as proof to all concerned that unanticipated changes, to which soldiers and Party secretaries must react, can force a redefinition of basic institutional relations. The formula of "Party leadership of the armed forces" no longer makes much sense in Warsaw—and, in principle, such a shift could also take place in Moscow if conditions warranted.

Let me now raise very briefly four current issues in Party-army relations, issues defined in part by the developments outlined above: political succession, personnel politics within the military, decision structures for national security, and economic change and reform.

There have been more Western misconceptions about succession politics than we can afford. In less than three years, three General Secretaries have died, the Politburo and Secretariat of the Party are quickly being brought into the post-Brezhnev age, and major changes are under way at middle and lower echelons. The question is, What role has the military played in these exciting events?

Many Western observers, especially journalists, took it as self-evident that the military played a major part in bringing Yuri Andropov to the Party leadership in 1982. It was sometimes concluded that the disarray in the Party leadership was so great that the military high command had become a kind of collective kingmaker, directly involved from now on in the selection of the top Party boss and, by extension, of great weight in the making of crucial Soviet decisions.

No convincing evidence was ever offered that the generals had exercised such influence either in 1982 or later, when Andropov was terminally ill. Difficult to apply to Andropov, the argument for military intervention in leadership selection is simply impossible to sustain when it comes to the accession of Konstantin Chernenko in February 1984 and Mikhail Gorbachev in March 1985. One would think that Chernenko would have been one of the last people that career soldiers would have wanted to see in this office. He had no prior connection with the military to speak of; he had not even served in the war, but had spent those years in minor civilian positions far away from the front. Neither before nor after his accession did he seem to address any of the issues that most concerned the military.

Nor is there anything to hint at real military influence in the choice of Gorbachev. A fair number of senior commanders probably would have felt more comfortable with Gorbachev's main rival, Grigori Romanov, a wounded war veteran who had been in charge of national security affairs within the Secretariat since June 1983.

Speculation was rife in the West about a supposed political vacuum in Moscow in the early 1980s. This was indeed a time of weak and uncertain individual leadership, but there is nothing to suggest that the collective solidarity or resolve of the highest councils of the Party ever wavered, or that Party authority was ever so much in question that there was an actual opening for military interference. The coming to power of Gorbachev surely settles the succession and leadership question for some time to come, and perhaps for the rest of the century.

There is an intermediate politics of succession, which concerns the filling of lesser offices and the dispensing of patronage and influence below the peak level. Here the military establishment is without a doubt involved at the present time— but mostly on the receiving end. There is no inkling of military participation in political deals that would result in military personnel being assigned to, say, major posts in economic or cultural management. But there are signs of intrigue and maneuvering involving both civilian and military figures and producing significant changes in personnel within the armed forces themselves.

The key to this kind of politics as it affects the most significant positions within the military is a top secret body called the Defense Council. This council, whose membership is never disclosed by the Soviets, includes no more than a handful of top politicians and a few of the most senior military officers. It deals, as best we know, with the most sensitive issues of national security, including, one presumes, appointment to high military office. The membership of the Defense Council (as far as we can reconstruct it) has been in considerable flux in recent months. In December 1984 Defense Minister Ustinov died, followed four months later by General Secretary Chernenko. Romanov, the senior Party secretary in the area and most likely a council member, was retired by Gorbachev in July 1985, and concurrently long-time Foreign Minister Andrei Gromyko was moved to the largely ceremonial position of head of state.

The Defense Council by July 1985 had thus acquired in only seven months an extraordinary number of new members: Defense Minister Sokolov; Gorbachev, the new General Secretary (who may previously have been a member, but of lesser standing); Lev Zaikov, the new Secretary for Defense Affairs; Edward Shevardnadze, Gromyko's replacement as Foreign Minister; and perhaps one or two others (such as Yegor Ligachev, the new Party secretary in the ideological realm). Midway through July 1985 the council made or ratified several significant personnel decisions that may soon be followed by others. General Aleksei Yepishev, chief of the political administration of the army since 1962, was pensioned off and replaced by a man twenty years his junior. The commander of the Strategic Missile Forces yielded to a somewhat younger man—one recruited from the Ground Forces rather than from the same branch of service.

There also seems to have been some change in the status of a very controversial figure, Marshal Nikolai Ogarkov. Ogarkov, chief of General Staff since 1977, was abruptly removed from this position in September 1984, presumably at Chernenko's behest, and sent to an undisclosed but lesser post. In the summer of 1985, rumor and certain pieces of Kremlinological evidence pointed to a kind of rehabilitation of the marshal, though not yet of his return to the heights from which he was toppled in 1984. The meaning of this change is hard to fathom. Of one thing we can be certain: that opinions on Ogarkov, an outspoken military professional with an engineering background and numerous Party connections, were divided within both Party and army. He may well have offended military colleagues by his frank comments on the need to update Soviet military doctrine and by his emphasis on the need to prepare for conventional rather than nuclear battle. It is to be hoped that further information will soon come to light on the intriguing Ogarkov affair, which may not yet be over.

Something should be said about possible developments in Soviet organization for national security. What with the changes in the Politburo and the rapidly evolving domestic and internal situations, the time may be ripe for institutional changes that would bring Soviet decision-making machinery in this area more in line with Kremlin requirements. The Soviets have inherited a rather archaic setup, designed to meet the security priorities of an earlier age, among them the need to assert basic political control over a hostile officer corps, to funnel military advice to civilian leaders under conditions of great secrecy, and to encourage the building up more or less from scratch of an armaments industry.

These objectives have long since been met. The world, meanwhile, evolves, and it is just possible that a new General Secretary and a more creative Politburo will be re-examining institutions such as the Defense Council. The Ogarkov affair, which clearly has been fought out with some real heat, may prompt this. Creation of an active Party department for defense and security, with some distance from the military establishment, would be a significant step. A more prominent role for civilian think tanks would be another. Appointment of a civilian defense minister from outside the military-industrial complex would be still another. The fact that Gorbachev could name a regional Party secretary (Shevardnadze) as Foreign Minister indicates that this last option is not impossible.

A final concrete issue demanding attention is, of course, that of internal reform, particularly in the economic area. We know that the Soviet hierarchy has been discussing, without yet resolving, the possibility of a far-reaching overhaul of the economy, with an eye to improving disappointing growth rates and increasing the regime's legitimacy and foreign prestige.

Where does the military stand on reform? The answer depends to some degree on what is meant by reform. If one is speaking of fundamental political reform—the abolition of the one-party system, the institution of competitive elections, civil rights guaranteed by independent courts—then most in the Soviet military would be opposed, as would most people with power throughout the existing Soviet system. The chances of any such reform taking place are remote. If, at the opposite extreme, one means by reform relatively marginal and tinkering changes, then most military officers will probably be indifferent but not opposed, much like most other members of the Soviet middle class.

However, the area within which the interesting debates are taking place, and in which the really difficult choices will have to be made in the years ahead, lies between these two extremes. Gorbachev has at times displayed some sympathy and support for economic changes that are now openly discussed in the Soviet press: greater wage and material incentives for employees; more room for private enterprise in agriculture and urban services; administrative deconcentration within industry; greater use of price and profit levers, particularly in the encouragement of technological innovation.

Here military opinion, so far as we can surmise from the fragmentary evidence, is split. The Soviet military contains die-hard conservatives at one extreme and a few radical reformers at the other. It also includes officers, especially at junior grades, who agree with Gorbachev on the severity of Soviet economic woes and are at as great a loss as he and the Politburo often seem to be about what to do to improve the situation.

It is most unlikely that the Soviet military is capable of blocking economic reform on its own. Nor is it likely to take the lead in the reform process, at least under present circumstances. (Things may be different ten or fifteen years from now.) What is conceivable is military participation in a pro-reform coalition committed to taking difficult and at times unpopular decisions in the long-term interests of the internal stability and external competitiveness of the Soviet system.

One can imagine that even a soldier of the older generation like Marshal Ogarkov (born in 1918) could be drawn into such a coalition. He has referred on several occasions to the need for a dynamic economic base to sustain military strength and technological innovation. He may be in a position to know better than an academician or a regional Party politician that, from the standpoint of national military power, economic stagnation will eventually have to be reckoned with, particularly if both the United States and China are dealing with the problem effectively on their own.

For the next few years, the military certainly can live with the status quo. The Soviet economy is not about to collapse, and the Soviet defense budget will keep on growing by inches if not by miles. But the danger in standing pat is that efforts to make the unreformed Soviet economy perform better will work against military interests. The military has done reasonably well in the unreformed economic system because that system functions through a ranking of priorities. Under the status quo the military effort gets the highest ranking, but the most common suggestion for economic improvement made by ideological conservatives is that further priorities—to be achieved by old-fashioned campaigns and drives—be added to the list. If everything becomes a priority, the military establishment, which once was almost the only priority in the economy, stands to lose.

THE DEVELOPMENT OF SOVIET MILITARY POWER

V. Kulagina, "For the Defense of the USSR," 1927

CONDOLEEZZA RICE

The growth of Soviet military power has been a source of considerable comment (and concern) in the West. In spite of technological inferiority and severe economic pressures, the Soviet Union has reached parity with the United States in most areas, and in some cases, surpassed us. When surveying the impressive scope of Soviet military power, four questions come readily to mind: Who decides Soviet defense policy? What is the composition of the Soviet force structure? Why have they acquired this power? And, finally, when looking to the Gorbachev era, can they afford to continue to acquire military power at anything approaching the current rate?

The question of who decides Soviet defense policy is a difficult one. The Soviet defense decision-making process is shrouded in secrecy, but it is possible to talk about the relevant bodies and to speak, with some authority, about how the process is supposed to work. The important bodies are described briefly in Figure 1. The Soviets say, and there is no reason to doubt this, that the Communist Party is the directing body in the defense decision-making process. The Party is said to "guide" the acquisition of weapons and to make all decisions regarding the use of forces. The use of the word "guide" or "direct" *(rukovodstvo)* means that the Communist Party sets the broad outlines

FIGURE 1

Organizational Chart of Party-Military Top Command

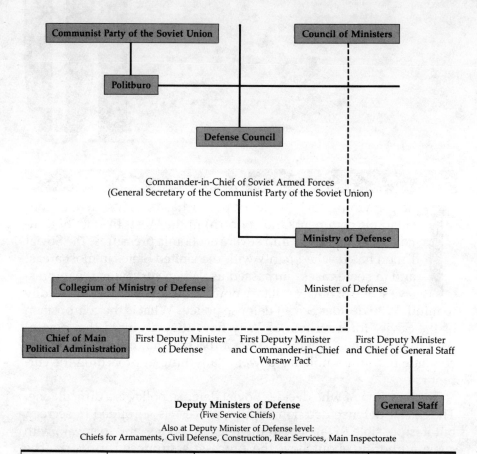

Communist Party of the Soviet Union

Council of Ministers

Politburo

Defense Council

Commander-in-Chief of Soviet Armed Forces
(General Secretary of the Communist Party of the Soviet Union)

Ministry of Defense

Collegium of Ministry of Defense

Minister of Defense

| Chief of Main Political Administration | First Deputy Minister of Defense | First Deputy Minister and Commander-in-Chief Warsaw Pact | First Deputy Minister and Chief of General Staff |

Deputy Ministers of Defense
(Five Service Chiefs)

General Staff

Also at Deputy Minister of Defense level:
Chiefs for Armaments, Civil Defense, Construction, Rear Services, Main Inspectorate

Commander-in-Chief Strategic Rocket Forces	Commander-in-Chief Ground Forces	Commander-in-Chief Air Force	Commander-in-Chief Air Defense Forces	Commander-in-Chief Navy

———— *legal and operational link*

- - - - - *link is more important legally than operationally* for defense policy, but obviously the Communist Party is a massive organization and cannot make defense policy in any real sense.

Even the Politburo is too big and too diverse to play this role. There are members of the Politburo whose interests and competence do not relate to defense. Consequently, the highest political authority in defense decision making is a small body called the Defense Council. This group is rightly considered the central, directing body in the formulation of defense policy. The closest equivalent in the United States is the National Security Council, but the Defense Council is probably smaller and seems to have wider-ranging powers and responsibilities. Its composition and routine are largely unknown. Most scholars assume that it is primarily a civilian body, though some would argue that the chief of the General Staff (always a professional military officer) is a member. We do know that the general secretary of the Communist Party is traditionally the chairman, and the membership presumably includes the minister of defense, the chairman of the KGB (the Committee for State Security), the foreign minister, and perhaps a handful of others. The Defense Council operates in peacetime, but it would be transformed into the directing body for the Soviet armed forces in wartime. The general secretary is also commander-in-chief of the armed forces in war and peace.

While the Defense Council sets broad policy direction, it cannot attend to the daily development of Soviet forces. This is the job of the Ministry of Defense, currently under the direction of Marshal of the Soviet Union S.L. Sokolov. The minister of defense has three first deputies. The first is an administrative deputy who oversees the ministry's work and acts as minister in his absence. The second, the chief of the General Staff, is the military commander of Soviet forces and an extremely important actor in the Soviet Union. There is no equivalent in the United States. While the chairman of the American Joint Chiefs of Staff simply coordinates the policies and requests of the various services (Army, Navy, Air Force, and Marines), the chief of the General Staff is the immediate superior of the Soviet service chiefs. He has enormous power in determining the structure and content of Soviet force posture and doctrine. The third deputy minister is the commander-in-chief of the Warsaw Pact forces—the unified alliance of the armies of Czechoslovakia, Bulgaria, the German Democratic Republic, Hungary, Poland, Romania, and the USSR. This alliance is roughly analogous to NATO, but the Soviets dominate decision making and have forced much tighter integration and coordination than NATO could ever hope to achieve. The Warsaw Pact forces are always headed by a Soviet marshal.

There is one other high-ranking officer who enjoys the status of a first deputy minister although he is not technically one. The chief of the Main Political Administration is in charge of a massive organization that parallels the command structure in the Soviet armed forces. Every unit within the armed forces has both a military commander and a deputy commander for political affairs. This system dates from the Revolution, when politically reliable "commissars" were placed within the command structure to ensure the loyalty of commanders who had largely been drawn from the tsarist army. Over time, as the military commanders became members of the Communist Party (at least 96 percent are Party members today), the need for "watchdogs" within the armed forces declined. Nevertheless, the system persists and political officers perform a variety of functions, including political education and indoctrination of troops, fostering a sense of Party loyalty and spirit within the armed forces, and, on some occasions, personal counseling and morale building.

The nerve center for the Soviet army is the General Staff. It is often called the "brain of the army" and enjoys tremendous prestige and power in the Soviet system. It is the primary body for planning and employment of Soviet forces. Service on the General Staff is both highly respected and desirable for career advancement in the Soviet military. The directorates of the General Staff span the entire scope of military policy: operations, mobilization, communications, external relations, military science, and foreign military assistance. While each of the five services (Ground Forces, Strategic Rocket Forces, Navy, Air Forces, and Air Defense Forces) also has planning functions, the General Staff is the key body and can ultimately rule against the services in the interest of a combined arms perspective.

The actual relationship among these bodies is hard to decipher. In part, this is due to insufficient information, but in any case organization charts give a somewhat incomplete picture of decision making. Personal efforts to circumvent these structures, as well as powerful personalities, can shift the relative balance of power between them. Nevertheless, it is possible to look broadly at the question that is a source of some confusion in the West: How big a role does the Party leadership play in the day-to-day management of military affairs in the Soviet Union? Since management of military policy has been ceded to the very powerful professional military bodies like the Gen-

FIGURE 2

Military Responsibilities of Key Bodies

Communist Party of the Soviet Union

(Socio-political side of doctrine)
- decides when, where and against whom to use military forces
- allocates resources to defense through role in setting budget priorities
- approves major weapons programs
- approves any changes in military doctrine
- develops Soviet arms control positions on basis of options and assessment of military and other advisors
- approves major personnel decisions in military

Main Political Administration

(Dual standing as Party Central Committee department and agency of the Ministry of Defense)
- debates and codifies ideological/philosophical principles in Soviet doctrine (philosophy of war and ideological principles of international politics)
- oversees ideological education of both enlisted men and officers
- probably some role in military personnel decisions
- represents sense of *partinost'* (party spirit) within the professional military

General Staff

(Military-technical side of doctrine)
- debates impact of changes in military technology on doctrine, strategy and tactics
- develops overall combined-arms (all service) strategy for Soviet armed services
- decides composition of Soviet force posture
- primary military advisors to Party on major issues
- wartime "nerve center" for direction and planning of military operations
- gathers military intelligence

eral Staff, does the Party have any really meaningful role in defense policy? There is always overlap between various bodies, but in order to tidy up the decision-making process, let me provide a figure (Figure 2) that roughly approximates the division of labor between Party leaders and professional officers.

Before proceeding it is important to clarify the distinction between Party and military that is being used here and is used generally in Western scholarship. Every high-ranking Soviet military officer, anyone who could be considered a key policy-maker, is not only a member of the Party but holds a high-level Party position. The Soviets speak of "unity of Party and army" and they practice it. For instance, all the first deputy ministers described above are members of the Central Committee of the Communist Party. Nevertheless, a distinction can be drawn between people who are professional military officers—those who have made their careers in the military establishment—and people who are civilian Party leaders.

Generally, it can be said that the Party is responsible for what the Soviets call the sociopolitical side of military policy, that is, the politics of military power. The Party assesses the international situation, determines the level of resources for defense, chooses Soviet friends and enemies, and ultimately decides when to use force. Moreover, the Party approves any major changes in Soviet strategy and doctrine—key weapons decisions, important personnel changes—and determines arms control policy. This is what is meant by setting the broad guidelines of policy.

But the Party must make these decisions on the basis of options formulated almost exclusively within the professional military. There is no evidence of wide-ranging civilian think tanks in the Soviet Union or of the involvement of academic institutions in the detailed debate of Soviet force posture and doctrine. The Soviet system is one that places a premium on the advice and expertise of the professional officer. Obviously, professional officers can disagree, and the Party is not therefore without options; but it does rely heavily on a relatively narrower set of options that have been debated and recommended through the central staff system. This is not surprising, since proliferation of institutions and bodies competent to debate defense options would also mean diffusion of sensitive information in a society that rigidly controls access to all information.

It falls to the professional military, primarily to the General Staff, to assess and debate the impact of new technologies on warfare, to determine what weapons to acquire, and to allocate resources among the various services. In contrast to our own system, service requests are harmonized into a unified plan before they are sent to civilian authorities, and there is some evidence that it is an integrated plan rather than the sum total of service requests. There is probably some tugging and pulling. If the chief of the General Staff tries to scrap a major naval program, the chief of the navy will undoubtedly fight back, perhaps even looking to his own political patrons. But the evidence supports the notion that the General Staff is quite powerful in this regard. Additionally, the General Staff, through its intelligence directorate, the GRU, collects intelligence on enemy forces and makes recommendations on arms control positions for the Soviet Union.

In wartime, there would presumably be tighter coordination between political and military authorities in a kind of super-command body. The advent of nuclear weapons has complicated the command and control problem and has given political authorities every reason to make certain that the decision to use "weapons of mass destruction," as the Soviets call them, will be the Party's. In the Soviet system, as in our own, the codes for the release of nuclear weapons reside with political authorities. There is some evidence that the coordinates to actually arm the warheads are passed through the KGB chain of command, while the command to fire the missiles is passed through the General Staff. This would provide maximum security against unauthorized release, but it is a very cumbersome system.

There are a few other key actors in Soviet defense policy. The defense industries sector, headed by a deputy minister of defense, is basically concerned with the weapons acquisition process and must work in close coordination with both the professional military and the economic planning apparatus. The KGB is, as noted above, important in the decision to use nuclear weapons. It has also been used to maintain loyalty of forces in warfare. There were NKVD (the predecessor to the KGB) people assigned to units on the battlefield in World War II who reportedly were ordered to shoot deserters on sight. That role has receded into the background, though defectors often note the presence of KGB operatives within the military who report on "anti-Party" activities among the troops. The primary function of the KGB in defense policy is in collection of foreign intelligence and in espionage. There is considerable rivalry between the KGB and the GRU of the General Staff. Finally, the KGB has special forces that it can bring to bear in a war situation for sabotage or assassination of leaders behind enemy lines.

These then are the primary bodies and their functions within the system. This decision-making structure basically leaves the conduct of daily defense policy to the professional military, with broad guidance from the Party's leadership. It is a system that has served the

Soviet Union well. Soviet forces number about 5 million and are equipped for every conceivable form of battle. Soviet manpower is drawn from a conscript system in which young men serve from the age of eighteen, for two years in most of the services, and for three in some specialized fields. By way of comparison, the American system is one of voluntary service and numbers about 2.2 million.

Soviet forces are divided into five services. The largest service is the Ground Forces, which numbers about 1.8 million, approximately one-third of the total military force. This is understandable as the Soviet Union is landlocked and, like the Russian Empire, has relied on ground power as the primary force. Interestingly, Khrushchev, challenging years of tradition, believed that nuclear weapons had rendered ground power obsolete. He summarily abolished the Ground Forces Command in September 1964. This powerful Soviet service, which had been the primary means of victory in World War II, did not go easily, however. It was not long after Khrushchev was removed that the Ground Forces Command was reinstituted.

The most important service in the Soviet Union is the smallest. The Strategic Rocket Forces (SRF) Command numbers only about 325,000. It was created in December 1959 specifically for the employment of nuclear weapons of strategic or theater ("operational" in Soviet terminology) range. Strategic weapons are those capable of hitting the homeland of the enemy, in this case the United States. The SRF also controls weapons capable of being launched primarily from Soviet territory to the European theater and whose range is over 1000 kilometers. They also control air and naval assets of comparable range. The rocket forces are the elite of the Soviet military. About 70 percent of their personnel are engineers and technical specialists.

The Soviet Air Force and Air Defense Forces, numbering 365,000 and 500,000 respectively, are considerably less important than the Rocket Forces or the Ground Forces. Nevertheless, in the generalized and comprehensive buildup of Soviet forces that took place in the late 1960s and early 1970s, Soviet airpower did increase considerably. At one time, NATO was thought to have vastly superior capabilities for air dominance, but newer models of Soviet fighters and interceptors are believed to rival American planes for performance, though they are not as dependent on high technology components. Even this is changing, however, as the latest Soviet fighters show considerable technological improvement. The Air Defense Forces are primarily charged with protection of Soviet and Warsaw Pact airspace. The Soviet Union, unlike the United States, has devoted enormous resources to defense against bomber and aircraft attack. The return on the investment, however, is questionable. The performance of the Soviet Air Defense network in the KAL 007 incident called into question the effectiveness of these forces when it took approximately two hours to locate and destroy a slow-flying, unarmed 747.

Twenty years ago, the Soviet Navy could almost be dismissed in any discussion of advanced capability. The Soviet Union is traditionally a ground power and the navy was always the stepchild of the forces. Under the leadership of the commander of the navy, Admiral S.G. Gorshkov, and with the comprehensive buildup of Soviet forces, the navy has benefited greatly. While the primary function of the navy's 425,000 seamen is coastal defense in support of ground forces, the modern Soviet Navy is capable of considerably more. It is the best coastal defense navy in the world, but it can conduct marginally effective anti-submarine warfare against American capabilities on the high seas. Moreover, it has a large and increasing nuclear striking force that can augment ICBM (Intercontinental Ballistic Missile) attacks against Europe and the United States. The latest generations of submarines are able to fire very long-range missiles onto American territory while sitting safely in Soviet ports, while other smaller submarines prowl just a few minutes off the Atlantic and Pacific coasts with missiles capable of reaching American territory in five to seven minutes. Thus while the Soviets still have an overwhelming amount of their nuclear striking power on land (over 70 percent), their firepower from sea is quite impressive.

Finally, the Soviet Navy has acquired capabilities for what is known as power projection. Power projection means the ability to go out into the open seas and to show the flag abroad. When thinking of power projection, the strongest image is the American Sixth Fleet, which has been used in numerous crises to signal American will and intent to adversaries. The Soviets are working toward acquiring this kind of power though they have never procured the huge aircraft carriers and accompanying battle groups to go with them. The problems for the Soviet power projection plans are many. Most importantly, they still lack effective overseas bases. They have tried, unsuccessfully, to acquire long-term leases for Cam Rhan Bay from Vietnam. Even in Cuba, a close ally, they face American power, which still operates out of Guantanamo Bay. This is a case where, starting late in the power projection race, they find themselves up against an adversary who has acquired assets and bases over a very long period of time. Power projection is also very expensive, and it is hard to protect the force against American countermeasures, which are quite formidable. As a result, the power projection capabilities have not developed as fully as might have been expected in the early 1970s. Soviet forces at sea are still best thought of as counterforces to the American Navy— forces which can make life miserable for the American Navy but which do not really threaten the supremacy of the United States at sea.

As befits a superpower, the Soviets have deployed their forces not only on Soviet territory but in far-flung corners of the world. There are 31 Soviet divisions in Eastern Europe (20 in East Germany, 5 in Czechoslovakia, 4 in Hungary, and 2 in Poland). There are between 100,000 and 115,000 forces in Afghanistan and another 25,000 advisors elsewhere in the Third World. These forward deployments and the sheer range of Soviet capabilities are impressive when we note that only two decades ago the Soviet Union could rightfully have been called a regional power.

There is no doubt that the Soviet Union is a global power in military terms. In some areas the United States has more capable forces; in others Soviet forces are equal, and in a few cases superior. As a rule, Soviet weaponry is less sophisticated than that used in the American armed forces. But Soviet technology is generally more than adequate to achieve the discreet military missions for which it was designed. Moreover, the Soviets are closing the technology gap in almost every area. They have everything from heavy ICBMs for intercontinental warfare to low-level forces for assassination and sabotage at their disposal.

This formidable force is not without its problems. First, there is evidence that the problems facing Soviet society as a whole are taking their toll on the armed forces. Alcoholism and lack of discipline are present among young recruits, just as they are in the work force. Second, the growing share of Asian nationalities means that the recruit classes each year are increasingly non-Russian. This has meant, among other problems, lower competency in the command language, Russian. The recently deposed chief of the General Staff admitted openly that this was a concern of growing proportion in the Soviet armed forces. In addition to problems among enlisted men, the Soviet officer corps is constantly admonished for a lack of creativity and initiative.

Just as in the system as a whole, there is a trade-off between tight centralization and direction and the need for flexibility and creativity in the field. Moreover, non-commissioned officers (NCOs), who are the backbone of any army, are said to be a weak link since they are often quite inexperienced and badly educated. One image of the Soviet armed forces that is becoming popular in the West is that of a huge machine that can function only from the top down. In wartime, the failure to respond to changing battlefield conditions and to show initiative would have dire consequences. It should be remembered, however, that in the crucible of warfare even officers who have been rigidly trained and punished for initiative rise to the circumstances out of necessity. Therefore, while it is easy to overestimate Soviet strength by viewing only the capability of the hardware, undue attention to social problems within the armed forces can give an equally skewed picture of Soviet power.

The most important issue, however, and the most difficult to answer is the utility of this power. After World War II, the Soviet Union could have justifiably worried about the ability of the United States to effectively destroy the Soviet homeland. The American nuclear monopoly and—even after the Soviets developed nuclear weapons—the superior delivery capability of the United States meant that the Soviet Union was vulnerable to a disarming first strike. Soviet ICBMs were very vulnerable and would most certainly have been destroyed. The Soviets' only deterrent was to threaten to annihilate Europe, using shorter-range nuclear weapons and overwhelming ground power.

Needless to say, the Soviet Union is in no such position today. Soviet forces hold not only European but American territory at risk. As a result, the present Soviet leadership has delivered something that the tsars could not: the promise that no rational actor could begin to entertain thoughts of invading or destroying Russian territory. The Soviets have effectively closed the historic route of invasion from the West, the Polish Corridor, through their political and military dominance of East Central Europe. Though a great deal is said about the "threat" from China, the balance to the East also favors the Soviet Union. One million Soviet forces are deployed on the Chinese border and the same theater-range nuclear weapons that are aimed at Europe, the SS-4 and SS-20, are deployed against China and Japan. The Chinese may be confident that their own nuclear forces can deter an attack by the Soviet Union, but under no conceivable circumstances could China contemplate aggression against its militarily superior neighbor. For a state with a history of invasion by outside forces this is a "good" that should not be dismissed lightly. The Soviets can obviously extend this "protection" to their East European allies. Any fear that the West might try to unravel communist rule in Eastern Europe by armed force is forestalled by huge conventional forces and a significant arsenal of nuclear weapons deployed in Europe and Asia.

The power they have acquired also allows Soviet leaders to break out of this essentially defensive, garrison-state mentality and to explore the utility of Soviet power in actively shaping international events. Soviet and Cuban power were brought to bear decisively in Ethiopia's war against Somali-backed rebels in 1978. An airlift, directed by a Soviet general and employing Cuban troops, provided the margin for victory. This is the kind of activity that Moscow could not have even contemplated fifteen years earlier. Then, in 1979, with the invasion of Afghanistan, the use of Soviet military power entered a new phase. The attempt to install Moscow's preferred rulers in Afghanistan and then, by using combat forces, to defeat their enemies was a new twist. The Soviets undoubtedly thought that their power would have been decisive by now. But an army trained to fight World War III in Europe has only recently adopted the tactics of guerrilla warfare. Soviet policy has been marked by incremental, tactical adjustment, suggesting that they are learning on the job. Forces have increased from about 80,000 at the outset to an estimated 125,000 now. Moreover, the Soviets have finally begun to employ search-and-destroy tactics against villages which harbor Afghan fighters and to pressure Pakistan, the Afghan rebels' safe haven.

The war has become a protracted and draining test for the Soviet armed forces. Nevertheless, Moscow shows no signs of leaving Afghanistan. The war is still being fought at what the Kremlin deems acceptable costs. Soviet casualties have been estimated at 20,000 to 25,000 over the six years of the war. There are scattered reports of crises in morale among soldiers in Afghanistan, and questions are finally being asked at home about missing sons and husbands. There is no evidence that any of these trends has reached a level sufficient to force a fundamental reassessment of the Soviet presence there.

The exercise of raw Soviet military power has been the exception rather than the rule. But lacking the economic resources to bid for influence in the developing world, the Soviets have attempted to use their military resources to gain influence. The Soviet Union maintains an active and costly military assistance campaign in the Third World. They have used these resources to help bring friendly governments to power and to secure teetering allies. The insatiable appetite of governments in the Middle East for arms has also been fed by a Soviet Union looking for a foothold in a region where it is diplomatically weak. Consequently, the Soviet military assistance program is a patchwork of cash sales for hard currency, support for friendly communist governments and national liberation movements, and arms to less than "progressive" governments who ally themselves, sometimes only temporarily, with Moscow against the West.

This less than coherent assistance program is easily observable when looking at the list of clients. In addition to arms sales and credits to ideological allies in Cuba, Nicaragua, South Yemen, Angola, and Ethiopia, and to liberation movements in South Africa and Central America, the Soviets support considerably less "progressive" but anti-Western governments in places like Libya and Syria and non-aligned states like India. For the most part, the Soviets seem to be willing to take friends where they can get them. Recipient states or movements receive both military hardware and advisors in most military assistance packages.

This policy has had mixed results. While arms sales have helped to increase the number of communist governments in the world, it has been considerably harder to keep them in the Soviet orbit. Moscow's meager economic assistance has led Angola and Mozambique to dependence on old antagonists. In Angola, Western capital continues to play the major economic role through Gulf Oil. The picture is even more dismal for Moscow in Mozambique, which is, if anything, more dependent on South Africa now than before the Revolution. In those non-communist countries which have been courted with arms, it has been very difficult for Moscow to dictate policy. The Syrian intervention in Lebanon in 1976, which Moscow bitterly opposed, is one such example. In two important cases, Egypt and Indonesia, the Soviet investment was simply washed away when these governments turned toward the West. The fact is that the complicated political environment in the Third World has been extremely frustrating for Moscow. But this point should not be overstated. Moscow is still relatively better off in the Third World as a result of its military assistance program than it would have been without it. Soviet power is not confined to the Eurasian land mass, as it was 30 years ago. It is just that the road to influence through military power has not been as smooth as the Soviets would have liked. What lessons the new Soviet leadership will derive from that experience remains to be seen.

Not surprisingly, the utility of Soviet military power depends largely on the political context. There is no doubt that the Soviets have achieved precisely what they hoped for in the matter of defending Soviet territory and their proximate allies. They argue that their overwhelming nuclear arsenal and impressive conventional forces were acquired largely for these defensive purposes. But one point is worth making about the "defensive" nature of Soviet military power in Europe. Soviet military strategy, as we have seen, was conceived by military professionals. Military professionals are charged with devising tactics to win wars, not to prevent them. While the sociopolitical side of Soviet doctrine is cautious, Soviet military strategy is undeniably offensive. Soviet strategy can best be summed up by the adage, "The best defense is a good offense." The Soviets make it clear that should war "become inevitable," they will make a full-scale offensive attempt to win. If the war is in Europe, they will try to press onto the territory of NATO to decisively defeat the enemy. More importantly, they will not wait to be attacked because, in warfare, the initiating side enjoys an overwhelming advantage.

For a very long time, nuclear weapons had little impact on this fundamental tenet of Soviet military strategy. They never accepted the doctrine of MAD (Mutually Assured Destruction), in which the threat to retaliate against cities was considered enough to deter aggression. They acquired forces, nuclear and conventional, to fight and prevail should war break out. Soviet political leaders, however, were always extremely circumspect about nuclear weapons and finally came to admit that prevailing and winning in a nuclear war had no meaning. This has led to refinements in Soviet military strategy that take into account the unpredictability of nuclear warfighting. The Soviet answer has not been, however, to adopt American notions of deterrence solely through retaliation. Rather, the Soviets have pursued a strategy to fight a conventional war and to do everything possible to keep it from going nuclear. They seem to understand that a nuclear war cannot be won, but they refuse to believe that the Soviet

Union cannot win any war which it undertakes. In this newer strategy, all the old notions of the primacy of the offense are in place. This means that there is an uncomfortable tension in Soviet military doctrine between the desire to avoid war at all costs because of its unpredictability and a strategy that places a premium on initiating war should (as the Soviets put it) "war become inevitable." The Soviets have been unsuccessful in resolving this dichotomy for the outside world. Perhaps the uncertainty in the mind of the adversary about what this tortured formulation of doctrine means is considered valuable in and of itself.

There can be little doubt that this strategy would be put into use if Moscow's vital interests were threatened. But what about the use of Soviet military power more broadly? We have seen that the 1970s did bring the use of Soviet power into areas of the world far from the Soviet Union. For such purposes they have acquired, at enormous cost, a wide array of forces. There has always been a tension for the Soviet Union between wanting stability and a war-free environment in the international system—so that the Soviet Union can prosper—and wanting to exploit leakage in the Western camp. The nuclear age has made the tension between promoting instability and desiring peace even stronger. Sometimes, when viewing the panoply of Soviet power, one is tempted to infer that the Soviets believe that enough power will overcome this problem.

In actuality, the Soviets have been very cautious about the use of power. This is a legacy that goes all the way back to Lenin. The idea that revolution could be spread by bayonet point, when tested in the 1920s, suffered miserable failures and consequently really died a very quick death. The alternative legacy bequeathed to Gorbachev is one that chooses opportunities carefully, knowing that political circumstances must be taken into account in pursuing military victories. The Soviets have a formula, a kind of measuring stick of how history is progressing, called the "correlation of forces." In applying it they are cautioned to take account not just of the military balance but of political, economic, and moral forces as well. They have a fairly clear view that military force applied indiscriminately in circumstances where other elements do not favor them is risky. That mind-set has probably been reinforced by the experience of Afghanistan.

The Soviets are finally able to do what is of primary importance to them. As Leonid Brezhnev put it, "No one can contemplate disturbing the Soviet Union's way of life." They can also exploit opportunities to extend Soviet and communist power in the Third World. But they will do that very cautiously, lest too aggressive a campaign to extend Soviet power unravel the security of the Soviet Union itself.

The Soviet Union has made great sacrifices to achieve the military status it now enjoys. It is fair, however, to ask whether the sluggish Soviet economy can continue to keep pace with the more powerful American economy. Mikhail Gorbachev faces difficult choices in resource allocation over the next few years because there is no evidence that the rate of growth in the Soviet economy will rebound enough to give the Soviets the luxury of unrestrained spending. In fact, the rate of growth in procurement leveled off in the mid-1970s and has shown only marginal increase in the 1980s. Nevertheless, it would be a mistake to expect the Soviets to view the gun-versus-butter trade-off as a dichotomy. Any military acquisition program has several phases. At one end is rapid acquisition of hardware based on existing technology, and at the other is basic scientific research that has long-term military applications.

There are those in the Soviet military who are arguing that it is really in the area of new technologies, microelectronics, particle beam weapons, and artificial intelligence that there is a challenge from the West. These people may be willing to forego short-term acquisition in favor of research, development, and investment in militarily promising technologies. Their time horizon might not be the same as that of those who wish to invest in basic research and to divert funds from military research, but it could bring about a temporary bargain between those who seek investment in technology for civilian purposes and those who seek the same for military use. In the short term, this could lead to a less intensive purchase of hardware and investment in future technologies. Then, should promised reform of the economy bring an end to the period of economic stringency, the Soviet military would be well prepared to acquire forces for the battlefield of the twenty-first century.

What is clear is that military power is too important to the Soviet Union to be allowed to fall very far on the priority list of any leader in the Kremlin, regardless of generational change. Military power is enormously important to Soviet prestige and position in the world. More importantly, the Soviet Union has always been a garrison state which believes that the best way to prevent war is to prepare for it. That essentially martial view of peace is not likely to change in the near future.

ARMS CONTROL IS BACK IN THE SOVIET UNION: WHERE IS IT GOING?

Poster from Hoover Institution Archives collection, artist unknown

COIT D. BLACKER

11

To answer the question posed in the title, we must first explore and define the relevant issues as viewed by each of the two superpowers. I shall therefore first highlight what appear to me the major points of controversy in the American debate over the role and purpose of arms control and then do the same from the Soviet perspective—that is, identify the most important issues confronting Soviet leaders as they consider the negotiation of limits on their nuclear weapons arsenal. Finally, I will conclude with a look toward the future: What are the prospects for some kind of an arms control agreement coming out of the negotiations currently under way between the United States and the Soviet Union?

To begin with the state of the debate over arms control in the United States, let us identify the three major issues and pose them in the form of questions:

First, what has been the cumulative record of arms control since the beginning of serious bilateral, U.S.-Soviet negotiations on the limitation and control of nuclear weapons in 1969? What have they accomplished?

Second, what has been the record of the Soviet Union in complying with arms control agreements, specifically agreements concluded with the United States? What does that record suggest for this country about continuing to honor existing treaties and accords to which the Soviet Union is a party and about concluding new ones?

Third—and the most difficult to answer—what is the preferred character of the strategic military relationship between the two superpowers?

Since the advent of the Reagan administration in 1981, these three sets of issues have been—and continue to be—of overriding importance both to the public and to policymakers.

First, on the achievements of arms control: The Reagan administration came into office in January 1981 with the strong conviction that arms control had been a dismal failure. The argument had two parts. The first, directed to the voting public, held that arms control, especially the SALT (Strategic Arms Limitation Talks) process, had failed to end or even restrain the nuclear arms race in anything like a meaningful way; that far from enabling a reduction in armaments and superpower tensions, arms control had in fact made things much worse.

Those within the administration making this argument held that the total number of U.S. and Soviet strategic nuclear warheads had increased fourfold between 1969 and 1980—from roughly 2000 on each side to over 8000. They went on to argue that neither the first nor the second strategic arms limitation agreement (SALT I and SALT II) had resulted in an easing of the nuclear threat. Quite the contrary; the prospect of war was closer and the threat to American security more pronounced, they contended, than at the outset of the arms control process over a decade before.

In other words, on both technical and broader military grounds, SALT was "fatally flawed"—a phrase used repeatedly by Ronald Reagan during the presidential campaign of 1980. Many Republican candidates campaigned vigorously against ratification of the SALT II Treaty on these grounds.

The second part of the argument, put forth less aggressively than the first, held that arms control had not only failed to make things better but in a perverse way had actually contributed to the relative decline in American military power and to the relative improvement in Soviet standing. Arms control had enabled the Soviet Union not simply to achieve rough military equality with the United States but to surpass this country with respect to overall capabilities.

Moreover, the argument went, as a consequence of their attainment of measurable strategic military advantage, the Soviets were now in a position to practice what was termed "nuclear blackmail" at U.S. expense. Since the beginning of the SALT process, it was alleged, the military position of the United States had flip-flopped—from a situation in which the United States was demonstrably superior to the Soviet Union to a situation in which it was demonstrably inferior.

The new administration therefore termed arms control on the SALT model counterproductive and inappropriate, vowing that it would not be pursued under its auspices, at least not until some changes had been made both in negotiating style and rebuilding the U.S. military posture.

There were still those in American politics and within the policy-making community who felt that arms control had not been such a failure, that on balance the achievements of arms control, while modest, were not unimportant. In addition, these people believed that the failures of arms control had little to do with negotiating styles or the relative decline in U.S. military power. Judging by the outcome of the 1980 election, however, it would not be an exaggeration to say that the case put forward by the proponents of arms control was not particularly effective or persuasive.

The defenders of arms control based their case on the proposition that the existing agreements, especially SALT I and SALT II, may not have been perfect, but that they were preferable to no arms regulation at all. They pointed out that progress on matters of such complexity and sensitivity was, by the very character of the process, slow-paced, uneven, and vulnerable to political developments external to the issues at hand. They failed, in my opinion, to make their case persuasively during the SALT II ratification hearings in 1979 and were no more effective during the next several years, up to and including the first twelve months of the Reagan administration.

Arms control had fallen on such hard times by 1981 that, asked when the United States might seek the resumption of negotiations to limit superpower nuclear forces, Secretary of Defense Caspar Weinberger responded that it might take several years to rebuild U.S. military forces to such a level that negotiations might again be possible and desirable. Essentially the same arguments were heard from Eugene Rostow, the first director of the Arms Control and Disarmament Agency under the new administration. Alexander Haig, President Reagan's first secretary of state, testified before a Senate committee in mid-1982 that SALT—meaning both the process and the 1979 treaty—was dead and not to be revived.

It was only because of articulated public pressure in the United States and a very restive Congress that late in 1981 the administration reluctantly agreed to return to at least one set of superpower arms control negotiations—those intended to limit the deployment in Europe of Soviet and U.S. intermediate-range nuclear weapons.

It was not until the midpoint of 1982 that the White House retreated further and decided to resume negotiations with Moscow to control long-range strategic nuclear forces. The point of all this recent history is simply to underscore the fact that the Reagan administration returned to the negotiations with great reluctance; it was a decision taken with genuine regret, as a consequence of forceful public pressure and a discontented Congress.

On balance, I would argue, the U.S. arms control proposals offered at both the INF (intermediate-range nuclear forces) and START (strategic arms reduction talks) negotiations were not designed to produce quick agreement with Moscow. They were extremely advantageous to the United States and extremely prejudicial to Soviet interests. Even the American approach to the negotiations changed from what it had been in earlier years, becoming much less flexible and much less innovative. These changes in style and substance were intentional, designed to give the Soviets a dose of their own medicine. It was also seen as a way to obtain a better agreement, the argument being that the Kremlin had obtained a beneficial outcome in both SALT I and SALT II by "hanging tough," and now we would do the same.

The administration also evinced considerable anxiety over the extent to which the Soviet Union could be trusted to comply with existing arms control agreements and whether they could or should be considered reliable partners in any future accords. The Soviet record on compliance constitutes the second major issue in the domestic U.S. debate over arms control.

This is an enormously complicated problem that deserves much more attention than we can devote to it here. In brief, however, it seems fair to say that many of the charges that have been made on this score lack adequate substantiation. At a minimum, they leave something to be desired by way of evidence. This is not to suggest that the charges have been made casually or disingenuously; it is to say, though, that many other people who have had access to the same kinds of intelligence data have not reached the conclusions held by members of the administration.

Between late 1983 and early 1985, the Reagan White House issued three reports on Soviet compliance and found evidence of Soviet cheating in a number of instances. Of all these charges, only three stand up to careful scrutiny—cases in which the evidence is convincing enough to make any careful, thinking person pause.

Two charges of non-compliance have to do with the SALT II Treaty, concluded in June 1979, but which neither side has ratified formally and to which neither side is therefore legally bound. The most the United States and the Soviet Union will say is that they will not take action to "undercut" the treaty as long as the other side demonstrates comparable restraint. Even though the unratified agreement "expired" on December 31, 1985, the commitment to abide by its terms will continue to be honored. The third case has to do with a provision of the 1972 Anti-Ballistic Missile Treaty (ABM), to which both countries are parties. This charge is a matter of some importance and complexity even though, as with so much in international relations, the matter is ambiguous.

The alleged violation has to do with the precise location of what is known as a "phased-array" radar. The ABM Treaty directs that any time either party to the ABM Treaty constructs a radar of this type (useful for identifying and tracking incoming ballistic missile warheads), it shall be located at the country's periphery and oriented "outward." The purpose of this provision is to prevent the deployment of phased-array radars that could be useful for what is known as the "battle-management" function. This concerns the effort to intercept and destroy missile warheads headed in your direction before they reach their destinations and explode on target. The purpose of the ABM Treaty is to preserve the mutual relationship of vulnerability to nuclear attack that forms the bedrock of nuclear deterrence. Should either the Soviet Union or the United States seek to defend itself against nuclear attack through the use of anti-ballistic missiles, the effort could upset this relationship and create military "instability."

For our purposes, it is important to keep in mind that the Soviets have constructed one of these radar installations in an area of the country forbidden by the treaty. It is, without doubt, a technical violation of the agreement. It is the clearest case, perhaps the only clear case, in which the Soviets have violated the provision of an important arms control agreement. Even though the violation is not, in and of itself, militarily significant at this time, it is a disturbing development and one that warrants very close examination and continuous evaluation. The Soviets argue that they are in compliance, that the radar is not for "battle management"; but the technical evidence indicates otherwise.

In response to U.S. charges, the Soviets have put together a list of American violations. They argue that not only has the United States crossed the line in certain cases with respect to a host of agreements, but that the U.S. record on compliance is abysmal. Virtually all of the Kremlin's claims are specious, the clear purpose being to keep pace with the U.S. in the game of charge and countercharge.

The situation has become terribly complicated and quite politicized over the last several years. The principal consequence of the dispute has been to provoke a U.S.–Soviet shouting match, with each superpower accusing the other of being a bad negotiating partner.

After the conclusion of the first SALT accords in 1972, the two countries established a mechanism, the Standing Consultative Commission (SCC), to adjudicate disputes of this kind. The SCC worked quite well during the first seven years of its existence. Many controversies were resolved to the satisfaction of both parties. Beginning in 1981, the United States refused to submit a number of issues to the SCC for resolution, claiming that the Soviets were not making a "good-faith effort" to clear up some of the outstanding disputes. The U.S. went public with a number of these charges in 1983 and has since gone back to the SCC in an effort to achieve greater satisfaction, while at the same time continuing to scold Moscow publicly. The Kremlin has not been amused. The problems persist.

The third issue in the American debate over the role and purpose of arms control has to do with the preferred character of the strategic military relationship between the United States and the Soviet Union.

I suspect that it will come as no surprise that since the late 1950s the Soviet Union has had the capability to inflict catastrophic damage on the United States through the use of its nuclear weapons. We, of course, have the identical capability. Moreover, neither country has the capacity to defend itself against the effects of these weapons. Both we and the Soviets are utterly exposed. There is absolutely nothing you or I could do at this moment to prevent our physical annihilation

DETERRENCE

in the event that someone in the Kremlin were to conclude that the time had come to go to war.

We can't run anywhere. We can't hide anywhere. We can't refuse to fight. We don't have the means to intercept incoming missile warheads. As individuals, we don't have the physical power to stop a nuclear attack. The Soviets find themselves in precisely the same situation.

From this macabre reality has evolved a relatively "stable" strategic environment. There is no incentive for either side to strike first, even during a crisis, because the side struck first will always retain enough retaliatory power to inflict what is known euphemistically as "unacceptable damage" on the aggressor. That means having enough leftover nuclear weapons to kill something on the order of 75 million Soviet citizens within an hour and their being able to do the same to us.

It means destroying two-thirds of Soviet and American industry in the same amount of time. It means having the power to poison the Northern Hemisphere's food chain and water supply, perhaps for generations. This is the basis of contemporary nuclear deterrence, which the strategic analyst Donald Brennan once appropriately described as "mutual assured destruction," or MAD.

At the conclusion of a speech on American defense policy on March 23, 1983, President Reagan made a plea for a new kind of strategic military relationship with the Soviet Union. "Wouldn't it be better," he asked, "to save lives than to avenge them?"

From this phrase was born what has come to be known as "Star Wars," and, more formally, as the Strategic Defense Initiative. What is important about the President's proposal is that it seeks to turn the existing superpower military relationship on its head, to invert it. Rather than basing our security on the ability to strike back *after* we've been attacked—after we've lost 75 million people, after our industrial base has been destroyed—wouldn't it make more sense to have the capacity to protect ourselves from such an attack in the first place? Why don't we develop the means to intercept arriving Soviet nuclear warheads before they have the chance to reach their targets?

The President's idea was not a new one. The United States maintained air defenses in the 1950s to shoot down enemy bombers. In the late 1950s and early 1960s we even built rudimentary anti-ballistic missiles designed to protect this country against the first Soviet long-range missiles. We all but abandoned those efforts during the 1960s because, given the number of Soviet ballistic missile warheads and the technical problem of locating and destroying these weapons, the effort was seen as hopeless. Cost was also seen as a major factor militating against the deployment of large-scale strategic defenses.

In the jargon of strategic studies, the military advantage was said to lie with the attacker. This meant that for every increment in defensive investment made by one side, the other side—for less money—could always add enough offensive strike power to render the defense useless. In a modern arms race involving competition between defensive weapons technologies and offensive nuclear forces, the calculation was that the offense would always prevail.

The President's vision, if implemented, would reverse the relationship between the nuclear offense and defense. This was immediately understood by strategic analysts and policymakers in this country and by their counterparts in the Kremlin. In addition, the Soviets claimed that this proposal was really designed to enable the U.S. to attain a position of meaningful military superiority and not, as the President alleged, to save lives. The Soviets reasoned that the United States might be emboldened to strike first, secure in the knowledge that its "Star War" defensive shield could intercept any remaining Soviet nuclear forces launched in retaliation. We might feel the same were the Kremlin to embark on a program to erect comparable state-of-the-art defensive capabilities.

Moscow's response to SDI (Strategic Defense Initiative), predictably enough, has been sharply negative and alarmist in tone. In part because of the President's support for "Star Wars," Soviet leaders argue that they can't cut a deal with the administration and that, as a consequence, no arms control agreement is possible at the present time. They denounce as a cruel deception the notion that the two superpowers can painlessly make the transition from a strategic military environment dominated by offensive nuclear forces to one characterized by secure and reliable defensive forces.

This is the third point of contention in the domestic debate over arms control—whether and how to accomplish the transition in strategic military policy from a doctrine based on the preeminence of the offensive to one based on the preeminence of defense.

How is this American controversy over arms control and military power perceived by Soviet leaders? First, it appears that the Soviets have come to the conclusion within the last several years that the present U.S. administration is quite serious about the effort to achieve military superiority.

The way they talk and write about this new American challenge is striking. They have begun, for example, to discuss the reality of U.S.

military superiority during the 1950s and early 1960s—something they had never admitted publicly until quite recently. Of course, they characterize that period as especially dangerous from the Soviet perspective. More importantly, they vow that the Soviet Union will never again find itself in that position—that Moscow will never permit the United States to reclaim its former status as the premier military power. But even the attempt to reclaim superiority, they argue, constitutes a grave threat to the security of the Soviet Union and the entire "socialist community."

Soviet spokesmen see two aspects to the threat. The first is what they regard as a comprehensive U.S. effort to procure a new generation of strategic offensive nuclear forces with the capability to destroy up to three-quarters of the Kremlin's long-range nuclear forces on the ground or in port.

Bear in mind that the Soviets place approximately three-fourths of their strategic offensive forces on land, in underground missile silos. Silos don't move around; they are stationary. And anything stationary can be destroyed by your enemy's missile forces. They place roughly 15 percent of their long-range nuclear forces on missile-carrying submarines, a small portion of which are on patrol at any given time. The remaining weapons are deployed with bombers. The United States places 50 percent of its strategic nuclear warheads on submarines, 25 percent on silo-based intercontinental-range missiles, and 25 percent on bombers.

From the Soviet point of view, it is easy to see why the U.S. strategic modernization program is so alarming. It looks to Moscow as though the United States is in pursuit of a "disarming" first-strike capability. With thousands of additional MX and Trident II nuclear warheads targeted on Soviet strategic forces by the early 1990s, the U.S. could have the capability to destroy in a preemptive first stike something on the order of 75 percent of the Kremlin's long-range nuclear weapons. This assumes that Soviet missiles would still be in their silos and their submarines would still be in port when the U.S. weapons arrived on target—a questionable assumption. Nonetheless, it doesn't take a Soviet sympathizer to recognize the potential seriousness of this problem from Moscow's viewpoint.

The Soviets were anxious about this situation prior to the President's "Star Wars" speech. The unveiling of the Strategic Defense Initiative made a bad situation just that much worse. Not only, from the Kremlin's perspective, were the Americans seeking the capacity to disarm the Soviet Union by striking first with their offensive nuclear forces, but they were also announcing their intention to explore ways to defend themselves—presumably against whatever retaliatory strike Moscow could muster following the initial U.S. attack. Such a development could place the Soviet Union in a position starkly reminiscent of the dark days of the 1950s, when even they admit the U.S. had this kind of awesome first-strike potential.

Consequently, Soviet arms control policy since 1983 has consistently emphasized that before any progress can be achieved toward the conclusion of a new agreement to limit the arms race, the United States must abandon its commitment to the development of strategic defensive weapons technologies.

It is the Soviet position that the United States must renounce SDI in all its dimensions—research, development, procurement, and deployment—before any serious negotiations can begin. The Soviets ask rhetorically why they should consider the reduction of offensive nuclear forces by agreement when they might need those forces, and more, to neutralize "Star Wars" and preserve deterrence. Why should they conclude any new agreement as long as the United States aims at nothing less than a first-strike capability? This, at least, is how the Soviets frame the issue for their own people and for Western audiences.

The American answer is that arms control on the SALT model hasn't worked and we need to try something new, even radically new. The administration argues that both countries should build strategic defenses and at the same time negotiate the reduction of offensive forces. With reliable defenses in place, the two sides can begin to drive down the size of their nuclear arsenals. Why have all these weapons if they can't be used? The advocates of SDI are proposing, they insist, a new form of deterrence, one based on the capability to *defend* ourselves against a nuclear attack, not *avenge* it.

The Soviet answer to that argument is that they don't believe it. They contend that, whatever the accompanying rhetoric, the U.S. goal is to acquire the forces to disarm the Soviet Union, to race Moscow in an all-out arms competition. The eagerness for a new arms race is based, they continue, on American confidence in its superior weapons technology and its larger industrial base.

It is important to keep in mind that in some sense the Soviets have no one to blame but themselves for this uncomfortable situation. In the ten years between 1970 and 1980, during which the United States exercised significant restraint in the development of its nuclear weapons capabilities, the Soviets accelerated their own programs in this area. They deployed a new generation of long-range ballistic missiles armed with multiple warheads. They deployed so many of these weapons that they came to threaten the "survivability" of the U.S. land-based missile force. U.S. ICBMs posed no such threat to Soviet forces. Even today, the existing American missiles can eliminate only a fraction of the Kremlin's ICBMs. Both countries modernized and upgraded their nuclear forces during the 1970s, but the Soviet effort was far more ambitious and comprehensive.

If nothing else, Soviet military activities during this time period did much to underscore the impression that the Kremlin had taken advantage of American complacency to transform the nature of the strategic balance and to obtain a degree of military advantage. As is usually the case in such matters, the reality is much more complicated than this characterization would suggest; it is debatable whether the Soviets achieved anything like military superiority during those ten years. What mattered, however, was not the truth but what seemed to have taken place, namely, the perception that the Soviets had raced ahead while the United States stood still.

I don't mean to leave the reader with the impression that one side is to blame for the arms race. The nuclear competition has always been an interactive process. At one time or another, each country has led the way toward the development of new weapons technologies. There were times when the United States has been more responsible, and there have been times when the Soviet Union could be held accountable. There is plenty of blame to go around.

What does this analysis suggest about the prospects for some kind of an agreement emerging out of the negotiations currently under way between the superpowers?

The first point to understand is that these negotiations are extremely complex—in terms not only of substance but also of structure. Prior to 1985, we and the Soviets had always compartmentalized these negotiations. At one point during the Carter administration, for example, we were involved in six sets of negotiations simultaneously. In 1982 and 1983, we sought to negotiate the control of strategic offensive forces in one forum, and intermediate-range forces in another. That changed in 1985. The superpowers agreed to merge into one comprehensive negotiating format discussions on both classes of nuclear weapons. We also agreed at Soviet insistence to consider limits on space-based and strategic defensive weapons technologies. The result has been to take what have always been individually complicated issues and consider them all together. This is unlikely, for obvious reasons, to simplify the negotiations. It is far more likely, in fact, to retard the process of reaching consensus.

As if the structure of the negotiations were not enough to dim the enthusiasm of even the most optimistic proponent of arms control, the negotiations also must take place in the context of severely strained superpower relations. This is the second point to keep in mind as we look toward the future.

The intense hostility that characterizes current U.S.-Soviet relations has interfered, in my opinion, with the kind of clearheaded thinking and dispassionate dialogue that must precede and accompany these sensitive negotiations.

It is very hard to imagine the circumstances under which any of us, as individuals, might enter into very serious negotiations with someone, if, out of earshot, your negotiating partner were accusing you of all sorts of infidelities, stupidities, and evil motives. Even though you might have a rational incentive to sit down and talk to him or her about a matter of common concern, it is only natural to be less than enthusiastic about that prospect when you're being called every name in the book. And that dynamic operates both ways.

We don't have to be friends with the Soviets to negotiate arms control agreements that are in our mutual interest. In fact, if we were friends, we would have no need for formalized accords to limit armaments. Each side must have some minimal level of confidence in the intentions of the other side. Both countries must believe that there is some conceivable outcome which, if realized, would be mutually advantageous. If the two countries are screaming at each other, hurling invectives, it makes the process of finding a common language just that much more difficult.

The third obstacle to progress is the continuing controversy over Soviet compliance with existing arms control agreements. It is very hard to imagine the circumstances under which the United States and the Soviet Union might conclude a new agreement in the absence of some resolution of this seemingly intractable problem. Moreover, the U.S. Senate, which advises the President on the ratification of treaties, is not about to vote favorably on an agreement as long as the suspicion lingers that the Soviets do not live up to their international obligations. To begin with, there is a substantial minority in the Senate that takes a dim view of arms control; to overcome their opposition, any new agreement will have to meet very exacting standards for verification. Those standards may well include provisions for on-site inspections—measures that the Soviets have always regarded as intrusive and a form of legalized espionage. The obstacles to arms control, in other words, are not only international in character, they are also domestic.

The fourth problem is what to do about the Strategic Defense Initiative. The picture here is not as bleak as it seemed even some months ago. The Soviets have indicated informally that they might be prepared to retreat from their official position of "no research, no development, no procurement, and no deployment." Specifically, they have hinted that they might be prepared to tolerate carefully regulated research activities in this area as long as the United States did not cross the threshold toward development and prototype testing. In exchange, Moscow might sanction a 50 percent reduction in the nuclear weapons arsenals of the two sides. Recently the United States unveiled its proposal for a 50 percent reduction in strategic nuclear weapons. The President, however, has been absolutely firm in his refusal to consider limits on SDI, pending the outcome of the research phase of the program. Nonetheless, a deal might be possible if both countries are serious about concluding a new arms control agreement and willing to compromise.

The final obstacle is the resistance of the two sides, at least up to this point, to engaging in serious bargaining. Washington and Moscow were no closer to an agreement to reduce intermediate-range nuclear forces when those talks collapsed in November 1983 than they had been at the outset of the negotiations two years earlier. That pattern continues. In the discussions since February 1985, no real progress has been made in narrowing the gap that separates the parties. The missing ingredient is political will. It appears that neither country wants to come to an agreement now—at least not an agreement that both would find acceptable—rhetoric notwithstanding.

It is difficult to overestimate the importance of this last point. The United States distrusts the Soviet Union and vice versa. We believe that Moscow is determined to attain military superiority. The Soviets believe the same about us. The American public supports arms control in the abstract but is generally unenthusiastic about the agreements that have been reached. Opinion surveys indicate that they didn't like the SALT II Treaty and didn't believe the USSR would honor its provisions. They thought SALT II forced us to "trust" the Russians, overlooking the fact that we had and continue to have the capacity to monitor compliance independently through so-called "national technical means of verification," mostly satellite reconnaissance. The Soviet public, much like the American public, wants an end to the arms race. But it is powerless to affect policy. Fed a steady diet of anti-American propaganda, they too doubt the wisdom of entering into binding agreements with their principal adversary.

We and the Soviets were not always so skeptical about the potential advantages of negotiated arms control. For a brief period, from the early to the late 1970s, political leaders in both countries looked to arms control as a way to lessen tensions and to moderate superpower rivalry. They began that process carefully, with small steps, and gradually expanded their efforts. Detente collapsed late in the decade for a host of reasons, some obvious and some less so. The lesson we should take away from that experience is not that detente failed but that, relatively speaking, it accomplished so much in so little time. That success was a direct consequence of political will, strong determined leadership, and painstaking preparation.

The November 1985 meeting between President Reagan and General Secretary Gorbachev did not produce any major new agreements on the limitation of nuclear weapons. That was not its central purpose. The summit might still be considered a success, however, if the two countries use the meeting to begin anew the search for compromise and agreement. The history of arms control should warn us against excessive optimism on this score, but not deprive us of hope.

THE SOVIET
ALLIANCE SYSTEM

El Lissitzky, *1923*

CONDOLEEZZA RICE

12

The leaders of the Bolshevik Revolution of 1917 did not expect to stand alone in the world for very long. The Russian Revolution was to be only the first salvo in a worldwide workers' uprising against the capitalist ruling class. It was not long, however, before ideological expectation and reality came into violent contradiction. Incipient revolutions failed throughout Europe, and the Bolsheviks were suddenly very much alone in the world, surrounded by hostile powers and subject to economic quarantine, German land power and, eventually, foreign intervention. The embattled Soviet state survived, but thirty years passed before the Soviet Union's isolation ended with the creation of the Soviet Bloc in Eastern Europe.

As a rule, it is better to have friends in the world than not to have them. In this regard, the Soviet Union is no different from any other power. Allies augment a state's economic and military potential and provide political support for foreign policy initiatives. But for the Soviet Union the existence of "friendly states" in the world has deeper meaning. Semi-sovereign communist governments, firmly tied politically, militarily, and economically into the Soviet web, are more dependable than transitory friends of different social systems. While it is possible to speak of Syria, Libya, and others as Soviet allies, it is useful to separate those relationships from others that have been more enduring and are buttressed by ties that run the gamut from similarity of political system to military alliance. Only a few states fit these criteria: the states of the Warsaw Pact and Cuba.

The center of the Soviet alliance system is Eastern Europe. The situation in Eastern Europe is, of course, the legacy of World War II, when the Soviet Army in its march westward liberated and occupied the eastern part of the German Reich, the former Axis allies—Hungary, Bulgaria and Romania—as well as Czechoslovakia and Poland, which had been allied with the West. With the Red Army spread across Central Europe, Stalin was finally able to deliver on the promise that "socialism in one country" would not be a permanent condition. The Soviets installed communist governments in Bulgaria, Hungary, Romania, Poland, and the eastern zone of Germany, and backed a communist coup d'etat against the coalition government then ruling in Czechoslovakia. By the end of 1948 Eastern Europe was communist and allied with the Soviet Union. The news was not all good for the Soviet Union in Eastern Europe, however. A split with Josip Broz Tito, the nationalistic and independent communist ruler of Yugoslavia, pulled that country out of the Soviet orbit before the end of the year. But World War II and Soviet military power finally delivered the Soviet Union from isolation in the world.

Eastern Europe is the region most vital to the security of the Soviet Union. It is important politically and ideologically, and it provides economic insulation from a world economy dominated by Western industrial powers. Militarily, Soviet dominance of this region not only sealed the Polish Corridor, the historic route of invasion from the West, but provided a forward staging ground for Soviet forces against the West. The thirty-one Soviet divisions in Eastern Europe are buttressed by armies in the small states that were sponsored and are dominated by the Soviet Union.

While Eastern Europe is a source of comfort for the Soviet Union, it has also been a continuous source of headaches. Three times since 1945 the Soviets have had to use force to remind recalcitrant allies that Moscow sets the limits of political divergence in the region. Moreover, ongoing economic, social, and political problems in Eastern Europe make it a constant foreign policy concern. These problems have led many in the West to ask whether Eastern Europe continues to be an asset for the Soviets. While the region still belongs on the plus side of the balance sheet for the Soviet Union, it is not the clear asset that it was in the days of Joseph Stalin or even Nikita Khrushchev.

At one time the Soviets were able to effectively exploit the economies of Eastern Europe to the benefit of their own. The advanced economies of East Germany, Czechoslovakia, and, to a lesser extent, Hungary and Poland provided a steady source of finished goods and industrial equipment in exchange for cheap raw materials. Agricultural products and refined raw materials were received from Bulgaria, Poland, and Romania at bargain prices. But in the 1960s, as inefficiency and waste surfaced, these structurally weak economies began to slow down. For the last few years the East Europeans have been as much consumers of economic benefit as providers in their relationship with the Soviet Union.

Cost-benefit analyses are very difficult to make because of lack of data and the peculiarities of pricing in the socialist bloc's economic union, the Council of Mutual Economic Assistance (CMEA). But it is generally accepted that the CMEA pricing system has shielded the East European economies from volatility in the energy market and in some raw materials markets. This amounts to Soviet subsidization of these economies. Moreover, the Soviets have been outspokenly unhappy with the quality of products that they are receiving from Eastern Europe in return for their support. The usually monolithic and placid facade of CMEA has given way in recent years to open recrimination and dissatisfaction with the state of economic cooperation. Nor is the dissatisfaction confined to elite levels. During the Polish crisis, ordinary Soviet citizens did not bother to hide their disgust with the Poles' fascination with Solidarity. They could not understand why, with product scarcity at home, the Soviet Union shipped goods and foodstuffs to mollify the striking Poles.

The picture is somewhat brighter for Moscow when we turn to the military value of Eastern Europe. The Warsaw Pact enjoys considerable advantage in Europe in conventional strength. The treaty provides the Soviets with legal justification to station troops deep into central Europe. Forward-deployed Soviet forces serve two important functions: They are the first line of military strength against the West and they serve as a constant reminder of Soviet power to recalcitrant populations or governments. It is useful to distinguish between East European territory and East European armies when examining the military value of the region, however. There is no doubt that Soviet forces in Eastern Europe are the best in the entire establishment and that, given renewed interest in conventional warfare, they would play the key role in any military action against the West.

The armed forces of Eastern Europe are a mixed blessing, however. While their loyalty will depend largely on the context in which they are used, problems of morale and a not particularly benign view of the Soviet Union have served to make them potentially less formidable than their fancy hardware would suggest. The armies of Hungary and Bulgaria are small and isolated. Romania operates virtually outside the Warsaw Pact structure. It has not allowed the stationing of foreign (read Soviet) troops on its territory since 1958 and has refused to participate in exercises since the mid-1960s. The armies of the northern tier—Czechoslovakia, East Germany, and Poland—which were dubbed the "iron triangle of socialism" by Leonid Brezhnev, are not without problems either. Czechoslovakia's army has recovered somewhat from the shock of the Soviet invasion in 1968, but it is not the elite army that it once was. Poland's military effectiveness must be called into question since the military elite has been preoccupied with running the country since 1981.

On the positive side, from the Soviet point of view, the East German army is efficient and cohesive, and has been helpful in foreign adventures. One might wonder whether the Soviets have mixed emotions about the presence of these virtues in the East German forces. Undoubtedly, the presence of 380,000 Soviet forces in the GDR (German Democratic Republic), outnumbering the East German army two to one, helps to assuage any fears of unwanted militarism. All of these armies have been affected by the economic slowdown in the region, and the Soviets have had to deliver equipment at basement prices to keep the quality of the armies high. It is estimated that the Soviets bear about 85 percent of the economic burden in the Warsaw Pact. This is yet another cost of alliance leadership.

It is important not to carry the balance sheet approach too far, however. The analogy suggests that states, like corporations, total up assets and liabilities. At some point, if liabilities are too great, a wise business person will cut losses and run. No one would suggest that this is in the cards for the Soviet Union, no matter how expensive Eastern Europe becomes. States, especially great powers, do not behave that way. Prestige and obligation are concepts that defy asset-liability calculations, particularly in an area of vital interest. The term "vital" denotes that it is integral to the health and continued existence of the core values of the state's own political system. Only with an understanding of the link that the Soviets draw between political dominance in Eastern Europe and the vitality of the Soviet political system can their fixation with the region be understood.

Eastern Europe was crafted in the Soviet Union's own image. There is no doubt that it dominates the region, yet it remains sensitive to any perceptible sign of political divergence in these small states. The fixation on orthodoxy seems almost irrational when viewing the spectre of Soviet power in Eastern Europe. Yet the Soviets' chief concern has been to keep the political systems of these states pure. This has meant an insistence on one-party rule, control of the press, and, to a lesser extent, state ownership of economic enterprises. It has usually been violation of one or more of these tenets that has led the Soviet Union to intervene. Many would argue that this is why tightly controlled Romania, in spite of her reputation for foreign policy independence, has been left alone.

But this desire for orthodoxy in Eastern Europe has often clashed with the desire for stable governments capable of ruling or, better yet, governing the indigenous populations. Nikita Khrushchev attempted to replace Joseph Stalin's occupation regime in the region with one that allowed limited divergence; it was cheaper and less troublesome to have governments in place that could rule effectively. The East European governments have, with varying success, tried to balance effective rule and political orthodoxy. Two trends that began in 1956 and accelerated throughout the 1970s have provided constant challenges to that equilibrium. Over time, economic divergence from the Soviet model has grown. This trend has been reinforced by the drift of the East Europeans away from exclusive reliance on Moscow and toward West European capital and technical assistance.

When viewing the economic systems of Eastern Europe, it is really difficult to speak of the region as a bloc. The constant has been state ownership of enterprises, but in Polish agriculture and small Hungarian enterprises, like bakeries, there is private ownership. Poland, unlike the rest of the Soviet bloc, never collectivized agriculture, and until the recent upheavals there, this system served them well. Most of the economic divergence has come as a result of economic experimentation. These small, weak economies were not able to muddle through like the larger Soviet Union. Only

Hungary took up the mantle of reform, however, and it stands as a shining example of a mixed system of plan and market. The stagnant economy of Czechoslovakia and the basket case that is Poland's economy are examples of what happens when reform is delayed.

It is not that these governments did not see the need for reform. Rather, they have been cowed by the inevitable link between economic reform and political liberalization. Czechoslovakia and now Poland know at firsthand that liberalization cannot always be confined to the economic sphere. Even in Hungary, where reform has come at a pace slow enough to avoid the provoking of a reaction from the Soviet Union, political reform has flowed from economic liberalization. Recently, Hungarian voters were actually given two or more names for political office rather than the customary yes-or-no-list vote. All were, of course, Party members, but in many cases the Party's preferred candidate did not win. As the Soviet Union turns to the issue of economic reform itself, the atmosphere for experimentation may become better in Eastern Europe as well. But whether these leaders will be bold enough to undertake real reforms and thereby risk political unrest remains to be seen.

Closely linked to economic divergence from the Soviet model is the drift of the smaller East European states toward reliance on the West for economic assistance. This trend began with Willy Brandt's *Ostpolitik* at the end of the 1960s and accelerated, with the blessings of the Soviet Union, during the generalized East-West detente of the 1970s. East Germany was the primary beneficiary, and its economy is the strongest in the East today primarily because of its special economic relationship with West Germany. The East Germans enjoy most-favored-nation trade status and extensive subsidization from West Germany. The price they pay is to allow more contact for families and tourists from the West with East German citizens. A part of the subsidization that the West Germans provide is channeled through West German tourists in what could be crudely called a currency-for-visitation-privileges exchange.

This extremely beneficial relationship—from the East German point of view—has led to a warming of political relations between elites on the two sides of divided Germany. Erich Honecker learned the limits of such warming, however, when his visit to Bonn was cancelled by a Soviet Union angry over West German support for NATO's missile deployment. Relations between Honecker and Moscow were frosty

for a few days as Honecker complied but was clearly embarrassed at being treated like a naughty schoolboy by the Kremlin bosses.

Other East European states have also benefited from the opening to the West. Hungary has taken advantage of the warming to sign numerous economic agreements with West Germany, primarily in the areas of automobile and aircraft joint-production ventures. Czechoslovakia has imported Western technology to shore up aging plants and has taken the opportunity to export traditional Czech light goods—crystal, for example—whose manufacture was cut back in favor of heavy industry after the communist coup. Poland and Romania used the opening to the West and the flood of credits unwisely, however. They now face staggering debts, which, at present, place them in a position analogous to that of many Third World countries. But all the East European states continue to court economic ties with the West. The fact is that the Soviet Union, itself falling far off the pace technologically, cannot provide the industrial equipment and goods that these states need.

The Soviet concern with orthodoxy is thus going to be tested for some time to come. The problems in Poland alone are severe enough to occupy the Soviets full-time. Certainly, the Soviets must be rather proud of General Jaruzelski, who came to power when communist rule was teetering, and managed to establish some semblance of order. Solidarity's organization has been broken and with it the threat to communist and Soviet power. The economic and social problems and the lack of legitimacy of Polish communism that caused Solidarity's rise remain, however. Nevertheless, the solution that the Soviets used did forestall civil war without overtly using Soviet forces against the Poles. But it must have been a distasteful solution that delivered Poland by means of a military coup. The Polish Communist Party still exists largely on paper and General Jaruzelski has given up his defense minister's post, suggesting that he and his military cohorts intend to rule for some time. The Soviets have never been enamored of powerful military leaders and they have been terrified of the potential for military rule. In fighting off divergence from the Polish workers they had to settle for both.

Whether Gorbachev will be more flexible is a matter for speculation at this time. He represents a new generation, but the attitudes toward dominance of Eastern Europe run very deep and are probably insulated from generational differences. It should be noted, too, that generational shifts are coming in Eastern Europe as well. Janos Kadar of Hungary and Nicolai Ceaucescu of Romania cannot be expected to rule much longer, and Gustav Husak's government in Czechoslovakia has lost many of the veterans of the post-invasion government of 1969. Kadar's skillful balancing act, Husak's "politics of forgetting" in Czechoslovakia, and Ceaucescu's independent foreign policy buttressed by a police state at home may very soon pass from the scene. This could provide a very fluid environment in Eastern European politics at a time of experimentation in Moscow—and creates a potentially explosive situation. Gorbachev undoubtedly knows that Poland and Hungary almost slipped out of Moscow's grasp in 1956, the last time there was a reformer in the Kremlin and a simultaneous shift of leadership in both Eastern Europe and the Soviet Union.

Certainly the tolerance of reform is linked to the economic reform in Moscow. The Soviet economy, groaning under the weight of East European dependence, would be helped by buoyed East European economies. Another variable is the state of East-West relations. During the 1970s, when the Soviet Union was preoccupied with its newly acquired global role, Eastern Europe was left more to its own devices in dealing with the West. Poland rudely refocused Soviet attention on the region, and the decline of detente seemed to put the Soviets into a "circle the wagons" mind-set. The Soviets obviously enjoy the game of trying to split the Western alliance but they will tolerate no analogous efforts within the Eastern Bloc. Divergence from Moscow's line can be encouraged by the West, but too active a campaign is likely to result in even tighter reins.

In spite of all its problems, the Soviet-East European alliance has been remarkably resilient. It has survived three interventions, a Polish military takeover, and countless other less traumatic problems. The alliance is well institutionalized through CMEA, which seeks, with limited success, to coordinate the economies of Eastern Europe and the Warsaw Pact—which has enjoyed greater success in mobilizing the armed forces of the region. This is thus far more than an alliance, because Moscow places real limits on the freedom of East European elites. The East European elites and general populations know that Soviet power can be used to enforce those limits.

The stability, albeit sometimes troubled, which the Soviets enjoy in their relationship with Eastern Europe is unique, but they have tried to build extensive ties with a few other states. The most successful effort has been with Cuba, where some of the conditions existing in Eastern Europe are also found. The Cuban revolution was an indigenous one and thus Fidel Castro does not owe his political life to the Soviet Union. But the Cubans have forged a fierce economic dependence on the Soviet Union, which undoubtedly limits their autonomy. The cost is believed to be 10 to 12 million dollars a day to the Soviet Union, but the Soviets have been more than willing to subsidize the Cuban economy. Like the East European economies, the Cubans are thereby sheltered from the volatility of world markets. This has been important recently, since the price of the primary Cuban crop, sugar, has been very low. On the other hand, the Cuban economy has suffered the same stagnation and inefficiency characteristic of Soviet-type economies.

Cuba, a member of CMEA, does not hold membership in the Warsaw Pact, however. The East Europeans have been insistent that the Warsaw Pact is a European security treaty, and thus any coordination of Soviet and Cuban military foces has been strictly bilateral. Fidel Castro and his brother, Defense Minister Raul, have also apparently resisted the Sovietization of the armed forces characteristic of the East European forces. Nevertheless, Cuban officers do increasingly attend Soviet military schools, and the Soviet bloc is Cuba's only supplier of military hardware. Cuba provides the Soviets a forward base of operations in the backyard of the United States. But, though almost 5,000 Soviet personnel are in Cuba, the spectre of American power in the region has forestalled development of Soviet offensive capabilities in Cuba. The memory of the Cuban missile crisis, when the United States was willing to go to war to prevent the installation of Soviet offensive missiles, has been sobering for the Soviet Union, whose forces are badly outnumbered in this region.

Cuba has been an important force in augmenting Soviet policy in the Third World. Though scholars disagree about the degree to which Moscow dictates Cuban action in the Third World, there is no doubt that Cuba could not afford its extensive activity in Africa and Central America without Moscow's help. The Soviet-Cuban alliance helped to bring communist governments to power in Angola, Mozambique, and Ethiopia. The Cubans are willing to fight in places where the Soviets will not use their own troops, and Castro is most happy to point to racial ties between Africa and Cuba to justify that action.

Soviet efforts to gain real allies rather than transitory friends have also extended to Afghanistan and Ethiopia. In the former case, the Soviet military effort there is an indication of how seriously Moscow takes its relationship with Afghanistan. In addition to the military effort, there is a massive aid program for the Afghan economy and technical assistance agreements to build up the infrastructure in that country. Afghan children are reportedly being sent to the Soviet Union for education as the Soviets try to install a sense of solidarity with the Soviet cause in the young. There are reports of similar activities in Ethiopia, but both relationships are relatively underdeveloped at this time.

One of the most promising alliance relationships was budding in Grenada before the American intervention ended communist rule there. The Soviets were trying to help the Grenadans to develop a Leninist party, central planning apparatus, and other trappings of the Soviet political system. But Grenada proved to be too far from the Soviet homeland and too close to that of the United States to provide a secure relationship. The sheer physical distance and renewed American interest in Central America may also explain Moscow's rather hesitant relationship with Nicaragua.

Eastern Europe, and to a lesser extent Cuba, will likely remain the center of Moscow's alliance structure for many years to come. As these relationships have matured, they have become more costly for the Soviets than they might have expected. But the value of allies cannot be measured in strictly economic terms. If there are choices to be made about the devotion of resources to helping build stable, pro-Moscow states, they are not likely to cause retrenchment in these key relationships. Rather, the Soviets may be more circumspect about courting new allies and new commitments. Attention and scarce resources could then be devoted to strengthening old ties. On the other hand, the Soviet Union is a great power and one which seeks reliable allies in the world. Should opportunities to build firm relationships appear, it is hard to imagine that the Soviet Union's leadership, albeit of a new generation, could resist the temptation.

A SOVIET MASTER PLAN?
THE NON-EXISTENT
"GRAND DESIGN"
IN WORLD AFFAIRS

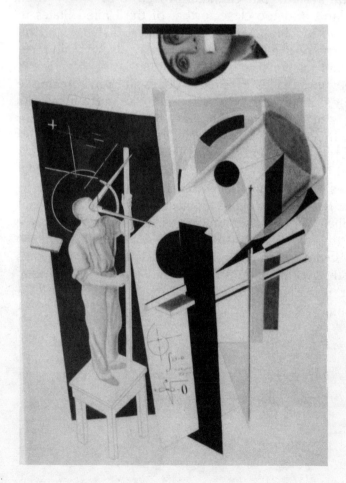

El Lissitzky, *1922*

ALEXANDER DALLIN

oliticians and high officials, including the current occupant of the White House, speak of a Soviet "master plan" or (to cite the title of a book) a *Blueprint for World Conquest,* to which the men in the Kremlin are ostensibly wedded. What is this master plan?

The short answer is: There is none. That is the view of just about all who have seriously studied Soviet affairs. But how do you prove that something doesn't exist? And how do you erase the imaginary existence of it from people's minds?

Attributing designs of unlimited conquest to the Russians is an old story. In fact, journalists and historians have been bedeviled for well over a century with fabrications intended to show such a plan. Perhaps the best-known forgery was that circulated in Western Europe in the nineteenth century as the testament of Tsar Peter the Great, who allegedly spurred his successors on to conquer India, of all places. That document was traced back to a French officer of noble origin and ideological mind-set. Other such "documents" attributed to Russia designs on virtually all of Europe as well.

This sort of output was probably prompted by Russia's growth into a major power under the tsars and fears of its further expansion. Actually, Russian expansion across Siberia and Central Asia over the last several centuries was not the product of any grand design, but rather the sum total of efforts by marauders and adventurers, local fur trappers and traders, landless peasants and individual military commanders, as well as of some annexations that resulted from wars with neighboring states. In that regard the Russian expansion eastward across Northern Asia was not so different from the American "conquest of the West."

By contrast with these fabrications, when it came to the Soviet era (after 1917) there was at least something authentic to build on. First the Bolshevik leaders and then also the Third International—the Comintern, which they founded in 1919—issued extravagant pronouncements calling for revolution the world over. It is this wishful and doctrinaire grandstanding that some Western commentators took for a master plan and sought to "expose" in books and articles for many years thereafter.

Such books typically abound in lurid quotations from Lenin and his disciples and excerpts from resolutions and proclamations of communist parties and agencies, all going back to the early years of the Soviet regime. But even the best informed—and this includes some who knew communism from personal experience—have failed to ask whether these statements have continued validity some sixty years later; whether Soviet leaders today actually accept them as guides to policy, let alone as a "master plan." And these, admittedly, are difficult questions to answer, as we have no way of probing the minds of Soviet leaders. We can, then, try to solve the riddle only by circumstantial evidence.

Moreover, even if Soviet leaders were to tell us that they still believed in these earlier statements, this would not constitute proof of a "master plan." Equally important, it would not prove that their formal adherence to inherited doctrine really shaped their policies or amounted to more than a ritual and a routine. If the notion of a master plan means anything, it has to be an explicit action program that its adherents must follow. Indeed, one of the proponents of the "communist blueprint" argument speaks of it as "the Soviet equivalent of Hitler's *Mein Kampf*."

Karl Marx had, of course, predicted the replacement of capitalism by socialism as an inevitable process everywhere—and first of all, in the most highly developed countries—much as capitalism had taken the place of feudalism before it. But in spite of his own involvement on the fringes of the revolutions of 1848 and 1871, Marx was not a man of action; he felt more comfortable studying in the British Museum than mounting the barricades. His writings did not amount to an action program. In fact, over the course of his lifetime he had occasion to change his own mind on many questions, and it is precisely because he left behind no "master plan" and because of the ambiguities in his legacy that disciples of very different persuasions could later claim his mantle and quarrel bitterly over the correct, or the only "true," road to socialism.

Vladimir Il'ich Lenin, in Russia, was one of these. When he and his Bolshevik followers seized power in November 1917, they had some naive ideas about the shape of things to come. They needed no master plan, they thought, because very soon socialist revolutions were bound to occur the world over, and therewith all conflict among states—and ultimately the states themselves— would disappear.

Initially they did not even anticipate the need for any Soviet foreign policy. When Leon Trotsky—later Stalin's rival and victim—took over as the first Bolshevik commissar of foreign affairs, he remarked that all he planned to do was to publish a few secret documents from the tsarist archives and then close up shop. What foreign policy could there be to deal with other communist countries among whom, by definition, there could be no conflict of interests?

It didn't take long before they discovered that their expectations had been wrong in a variety of ways; that other countries were not going communist on their own; that the new Soviet state did need to have relations with foreign powers. And, in fact, they began applying one political strategy after another to deal with the outside world, rejecting each formula once they realized that it, too, was based on erroneous assumptions.

Soviet Russia was weak, embattled, and without allies in those early years of its existence, and it was to be expected that the men in the Kremlin would count on the crucial help of fellow communists to stage revolutions in their own countries and thus bail the Russians out.

But, as a matter of fact, none of the revolutions abroad succeeded, even with Soviet advice, money, direction, or help. If the plan for communist victories in each country—by the local revolutionaries, and if necessary with an assist from abroad—did indeed appear to be something of a "blueprint," very soon it turned out that there was less to it than met the eye.

To be sure, the Communist International engaged throughout the 1920s in earnest debates over such questions as what constituted a revolutionary situation and where the revolution would come next. As late as 1927 two volumes of such debates were produced under the title, *The Itinerary of World Revolution*. Looking back today, it is worth noting not only that this was not a master plan for Soviet action, but that none of the places where Soviet-supported revolutions have taken place in recent years was even mentioned at the time. In those discussions you will find neither Cuba nor Angola, neither Kampuchea nor Ethiopia, neither Grenada nor Afghanistan.

Instead they focused on Great Britain, which in 1926 had experienced a communist-backed general strike that, briefly and mistakenly, buoyed Soviet hopes; on China, where the Nationalists were about to turn on their communist allies and all but wipe them out for some years—and on Soviet Russia itself. This indeed was characteristic. As hopes for revolution abroad proved, time after time, to be misplaced, what remained was the Soviet state.

In the end there was not a single successful communist revolution anywhere during the entire period of the Comintern's existence (it was dissolved in 1943, during World War II), and Stalin became quite scornful of the comrades abroad who couldn't fight their way out of a paper bag. Soviet Russia turned to building up its own military and industrial strength, ruthlessly and in a hurry. And the quip in Moscow around 1930 was, characteristically, that one tractor is worth more than ten foreign communists.

The rhetoric of world revolution continued to be mouthed, as were so many other things that in the Stalin days no one believed and no one dared question. If we accept the argument that the communist expectation of world revolution amounted to a political blueprint, we must also conclude that this "master plan" died when nobody was looking, and Moscow failed to report its demise.

What has happened to the notion of "world revolution"? The dominant feeling among Soviet observers is that "you can't get there from here." For whatever reasons, things haven't worked out as expected. A group of Moscow State University students, when asked what they thought of the notion of communist world revolution, shuffled their feet and giggled in embarrassment. There is profound Soviet disappointment with the communist "world movement" (which, in fact, has long ceased being a single movement, what with Stalin's split with Tito, the Sino-Soviet conflict, and the many other rifts between

Moscow and foreign communist parties, such as the Italian, the Spanish, and the Japanese). Today feelings of national pride are far easier to touch than are echoes of "proletarian international solidarity."

Ironically, new communist regimes came into being only after the Comintern was dissolved and, in many cases, they were established by force of arms from abroad, not by authentic revolution. This shift from banking on indigenous revolutions to relying on Soviet armed force was but one example of a fundamental shift in Soviet strategy, which belies the notion of any operative master plan.

While in actual policy Soviet state interests (as interpreted in Moscow) have invariably prevailed over "revolutionary" goals, the tired reiteration of obligatory revolutionary verbiage continues—as a ritual, as a not very effective propaganda theme, perhaps as a distant vision, but surely not as a prescription for action. With time it became clear, first, that the vision of a communist world has no identifiable, single set of operational implications for Soviet policy, and second, that the saliency of that utopia has markedly declined.

Paradoxically, when Moscow had a global revolutionary vision, it lacked the capability to bring it about. By the time it had acquired the capacity to make a credible claim to superpower status, its world view had changed in significant ways. As an American elder statesman said with regard to the aged Soviet leader a couple of years ago, "When I get up in the morning, I don't feel very revolutionary either."

What we find then is that over time the policymakers in Moscow have been obliged—generally without advertising the nature of their deliberations—to reconsider in fundamental ways both some of their expectations and their worldwide political strategy. Even if there had been a genuine master plan, it could scarcely have survived the many shifts in Soviet perceptions, perspectives, and priorities.

From Marx to Lenin the emphasis shifted drastically from a faith in the inevitable unfolding of history, stage by stage, to a celebration of will and organization. After 1917, as we saw, the notion of imminent world revolution yielded to the vision of a slower, gradual transformation. Even this prospect receded before the reality of a single communist-ruled state. Instead of the initial Marxian vision of grassroots revolutions, Moscow opted for revolutions imposed from above.

Instead of authentic movements, it went for revolutions imported from outside.

From the initial Marxist axiom of revolutions by "toiler" majorities in the most highly industrialized countries, the Bolsheviks shifted to expecting revolutions by organized minority movements, first in a few Western countries such as Germany, later—in a total reversal that proved realistic but required jettisoning much ideological baggage—in more "backward" areas, be it China or Albania, South Yemen or Afghanistan. For an allegedly "proletarian" movement, it meant focusing on countries where there was virtually no working class.

As we have seen, the Kremlin's political objectives veered from revolution abroad to the aggrandizement of the Soviet state. But instead of continuing the practice of incorporating neighboring territories such as the Baltic States into the USSR, after World War II the Soviet Union shifted to creating a belt of formally independent satellite states.

In seeking to consolidate control abroad—notably, in Eastern Europe—Soviet strategies have shifted from the use of mass terror to economic means, to political education, and to reliance on military power. In foreign policy they have alternated between self-isolation and alliance strategies, between anti-imperialism and the (failed) attempt at superpower condominium. Today the Soviet Union commands attention, fear, or respect, first of all because of its military power. This is a development that would have astounded the "old Bolsheviks" of pre-revolutionary vintage and remains hard to square with the canons of "classical" Marxism-Leninism.

Many things have happened that Soviet analysts had not expected. Even worse from their perspective, many events have been impossible to square with what Moscow had assumed was bound to occur. Time and again this has meant, for the policymakers and their advisers, going back to the drawing board.

The failure of communist revolutions outside of Russia was only one such cluster of miscalculations. Later, in 1931–33, the faith that Nazism as the "highest stage of capitalism" was bound to be the prelude to communist victory—that the road to communism led through Hitler—proved to be a suicidal delusion. Likewise, the severe splits within the communist world after World War II had, of course, been totally unforeseen and impossible to explain in orthodox Leninist terms.

According to Khrushchev, the Third World was bound to line up with Moscow as a matter of its own interest, but it just didn't happen that way. In fact, much of the history of Soviet influence in the developing world is the tale of clients and allies who got away—from Guinea, Ghana, and Mali to Indonesia, which until 1965 had been a major recipient of Soviet aid; from Algeria and Somalia to the Sudan and Iraq; and, perhaps the prime example (other than the break with China), the political defection of Egypt under Anwar el-Sadat from the pro-Soviet side. Almost invariably these were countries the United States had been prepared to write off as "lost."

Moscow has been no less surprised by the resistance it has encountered from its neighbor states—Finland, Iran, and Afghanistan. Even more serious, most Soviet observers were shocked by the collapse of Soviet-American detente in the 1970s after they had come to accept it as an irreversible product of American (as well as Soviet) self-interest. Sometimes, to be sure, there have also been pleasant surprises. Cuba, though a mixed blessing for Moscow, was one such unexpected windfall for the Soviet side. But whatever the surprises, their roster is incompatible with the notion of a "scientific" master plan.

I f the Kremlin's officials were merely foot soldiers in the service of a grand design, there should not be, in the Soviet elite or in the expert community, any disputes over foreign policy strategies. Yet, couched in the peculiar language in which such differences may be voiced, "how to deal with the outside world" has been a virtually perennial subject of dispute in Soviet elite politics and among experts advising those at the top.

From its earliest days, when the Bolsheviks were split over making peace with the German "class enemies" by means of the Treaty of Brest-Litovsk in March 1918, to the arguments in the 1970s over Soviet-American detente (had the imperialist beast really changed its spots?), foreign policy has been a bone of contention. Should the Soviet bloc go it alone against all "capitalist" powers or should Moscow try to divide the hostile imperialist world—with Germany against the Western democracies (as was the practice in the 1920s), or with the West against Germany (as was tried, intermittently, in the Hitler days)? Could the newly emerging countries of the Third World be written off as a sham and a farce (as Stalin thought), or was the Third World the locus of the "reserve of the revolution" (as Khrushchev was tempted to argue), or even its "storm center" (as Mao would plead)?

Should the Soviet Union seek to align itself with the United States against a hostile and militant China, or should it try to strike a deal to normalize relations with Beijing to block a more threatening Washington? Better an American presence in Western Europe than a nuclear West Germany, or better a benign and neutralized Western Europe than a NATO confronting the USSR? Was the first priority in 1983–84 an arms control treaty with the U.S., or was it doing nothing that would strengthen the chances of Ronald Reagan's re-election? Did the profound commitment to "progressive" change abroad continue to be valid, or did the Soviet Union now, in the nuclear age, perceive a paramount interest in stabilizing the superpower relationship in a new world-order structure?

In the arguments between optimists and pessimists in Moscow, is the Soviet Union forging ahead and is history going its way, or is it still (or again?) battling uphill, against heavy odds, against superior Western and Japanese technology, organization, and output? Can the Soviet Union rely on its allies, or is it the case that (as a senior Soviet adviser remarked) "we have no friends anywhere"?

The answers to all these questions have not been self-evident. The world has turned out to be so much more complex and intractable than earlier generations of Soviet leaders had expected, so much more varied and difficult to understand, that the one and only truth (which they claim as their monopoly) that had once seemed clear and obvious has become elusive and contested and hard to find. Even if there is a consensus among the Soviet elite on many of their core values, the differences—both on goals and on how to attain them—are substantial, and we ignore them at our own peril. If anything, the new generation now in power, as represented by Mikhail Gorbachev, is even less wedded to the old stereotypes than were their predecessors.

I s there something wrong with our own vision? We repeatedly impute to the Soviets a broader design than they in fact possess. When the North Koreans invaded the South in June 1950, we assumed it was Stalin who wanted to use South Korea as a springboard to Japan. It became clear, years later, that there was no such plan. When Soviet influence grew in Iraq, Syria, and Egypt in the late 1960s, American and British military analysts concluded that Moscow had given priority to securing a "land bridge" to Africa that would then be continued south across the continent toward southern Africa. This turned out to be sheer fantasy.

When in 1979–80 Soviet troops invaded Afghanistan, a number of highly respected American analysts, in and out of the government, concluded that the point of the invasion was to strike, through Afghanistan, at the Persian Gulf. It soon became clear that the Soviet move was prompted primarily by events within Afghanistan to which Moscow determined it had to respond or else lose control or, at the very least, face.

In each case we interpreted a discrete move to be part of a broader Soviet design. None of this has proven accurate, but the sense of a "blueprint" persists nonetheless. To recognize this does not make the Soviets nice, restrained, or easy to deal with, but it does make us wrong.

What is true is that there is generally in Soviet foreign policy more consistency than in ours. In part this is a result of the continuity of personnel on their part; Andrei Gromyko was foreign minister for a whole generation, during which he saw at least eight American secretaries of state come and go; and Ambassador Dobrynin, the dean of the Washington diplomatic corps, has been on the job in the nation's capital longer than most members of Congress or most representatives of the "fourth estate." Contrast this with the discontinuities on our side, which keep producing zigzags, reversals, and contradictions in policy. This problem should not be too difficult to take care of—for instance, by establishing permanent undersecretaries of state, on the British model—but in any case it tells us nothing about Soviet motives or intentions. No doubt there are other sources of Soviet consistency as well, such as their political and bureaucratic culture, but their impact is so vague as to defy practical application.

To assume the existence of a prior blueprint that guides Soviet policymakers is to divert ourselves from a serious understanding of the policy process in Moscow. As far as we know, broad Soviet policy decisions are made by the Politburo on the basis of options submitted by the Party's Central Committee staff, with papers and memoranda (where appropriate) from consultants and experts—such as the Academy of Sciences' relevant institutes—commissioned for the occasion, sometimes with recommendations attached for discussion by the Politburo.

Likewise, "inside sources" available to us give no support whatever to the notion of any grand design. If we take a look at the whole array of materials—such as Nikita Khrushchev's extensive memoirs, tape-recorded after his fall from power; or the Penkovsky Papers, based on the reports and debriefings of Colonel Oleg Penkovsky when he was working as a secret agent for the West (until the Russians exposed and executed him); or Arkady Shevchenko's recent memoirs; or the accounts of Poles, Czechs, Hungarians, and Chinese who had occasion to observe the Soviet leadership in action; or the memoirs of former communists, such as the Yugoslav leader Milovan Djilas, who later recorded his *Conversations with Stalin*; or the record of visits of Egyptian diplomats and officials to the Kremlin—none of them even seriously considers such a possibility.

We often tend to endow the adversary with greater power, skill, purpose, and wisdom than is warranted. On the one hand, this involves blindly accepting Soviet propaganda claims about the "scientific" nature of their policies—a self-serving political charade on their part. They have a stake in conveying to us, and to others at home and abroad, an impression of omniscience and infallibility, for which they can find rhetorical, if spurious, grounds in Marxist writings. By contrast, we have an interest in knowing the differences and hesitations and changes in outlook among them and, insofar as we can, in taking advantage of them.

On the other hand, attributing scientific omniscience to the Soviet leaders is at times calculated to make it easier for us to mobilize ourselves and our allies against the seemingly more formidable foe. This practice really tells more about ourselves than about the Soviet Union and amounts to a disservice to rational policy.

The weight of evidence, by a variety of indirect indicators, thus leads us to dismiss the notion of a master plan. But to conclude that there is no blueprint in the Kremlin is not necessarily reassuring. It does not reduce Soviet military power by a single warhead. It does not raise the IQ or insight of Soviet (or for that matter, American) decision makers by even one point. It does not reduce the dangers of nuclear confrontation one iota. Nor does it assure Soviet moderation or good sense.

To say that there is no master plan by which Soviet behavior is determined implies that Moscow's policies are marked by at least some flexibility and opportunism. If true, this may be far more advantageous to the Soviet system than rigid adherence to outdated schemes or goals and may also be advantageous to us, because it also means that Soviet behavior can be influenced.

To dismiss the notion of a Soviet master plan means to dispose of one of the most pernicious misconceptions we have entertained in regard to the Soviet adversary. Like our own, Soviet policymaking is influenced by interests and inertia; shaped by personalities, passions, and perceptions; affected by buck-passing and bureaucracy. Like us, Soviet decision makers are capable of learning—though they probably resist it even more than we do and learn even more imperfectly and selectively. Yet they can and do change; the notion of the immutability of Soviet outlook and behavior is another in the catalog of myths we ought to get rid of.

The fate of Soviet-American relations is not in our stars, nor is it doomed in advance by Moscow's irremediable commitment to a master plan. Though burdened and constrained in innumerable ways, it is ultimately subject to the will of those, on both sides, who shape their countries' destinies.

RECOMMENDED READING

Bergson, A. and H.S. Levine, eds. *The Soviet Economy: Toward the Year 2000*. Winchester, Massachusetts: Allen & Unwin, 1985.

Bialer, Seweryn. *Stalin's Successors: Leadership, Stability and Change in the Soviet Union*. New York: Cambridge University Press, 1980.

Byrnes, Robert F., ed. *After Brezhnev: Sources of Soviet Conduct in the 1980s*. Bloomington: Indiana University Press, 1983.

Cohen, S.F. *Rethinking the Soviet Experience: Politics and History Since 1917*. New York: Oxford University Press, 1985.

Colton, Timothy. *The Dilemma of Reform in the Soviet Union*. New York: Council on Foreign Relations, 1984.

Cracraft, James., ed. *The Soviet Union Today: An Interpretive Guide*. Chicago: Educational Foundation for Nuclear Science, 1983.

Gaddis, John L. *Strategies of Containment: A Critical Appraisal of Postwar American National Security Policy*. New York: Oxford University Press, 1982.

Garrison, Mark and Abbot Gleason, eds. *Shared Destiny: Fifty Years of Soviet-American Relations*. Boston: Beacon Press, 1985.

George, Alexander L., ed. *Managing U.S.-Soviet Rivalry: Problems of Crisis Prevention*. Boulder: Westview Press, 1983.

Ginzburg, Eugenia S. *Journey into the Whirlwind*. Tr. by Paul Stevenson and Max Hayward. San Diego: Harcourt Brace Jovanovich, 1975.

Hoffmann, Erik and Robbin F. Laird, eds. *The Soviet Polity in the Modern Era*. Hawthorne, New York: Aldine Publishing, 1984.

Holloway, David. *The Soviet Union and the Arms Race*. New Haven: Yale University Press, 1984.

Kaiser, Robert G. *Russia*. New York: Washington Square Press, 1984.

Kennan, George F. *Russia and the West Under Lenin and Stalin*. Boston: Little Brown, 1961.

Khrushchev, Nikita. *Khrushchev Remembers*. Boston: Little Brown, 1970.

Lee, Andrea. *Russian Journal*. New York: Random House, 1981.

Matthews, Mervyn. *Privilege in the Soviet Union*. Winchester, Massachusetts: Allen & Unwin, 1978.

Meyer, Alfred G. *Communism*. New York: Random House, 1984.

Nogee, Joseph L. and Robert H. Donaldson. *Soviet Foreign Policy Since World War II*. Elmsford, New York: Pergamon Press, 1984.

Nove, Alec. *The Soviet Economic System*. Winchester, Massachusetts: Allen & Unwin, 1981.

Pankhurst, Jerry and Michael P. Sacks, eds. *Contemporary Soviet Society: Sociological Perspectives*. New York: Praeger Publications, 1980.

Pond, Elizabeth. *From the Yaroslavsky Station: Russia Perceived*. New York: Universe Books, 1984.

Smith, Hedrick. *The Russians*. New York: Quadrangle/New York Times Book Co., 1976.

Solzhenitsyn, Alexander. *Cancer Ward*. New York: Dell Publishing Company, 1968.

———. *The First Circle*. New York: Bantam Books, 1976.

Tokes, Randolf L., ed. *Dissent in the USSR: Politics, Ideology and People*. Baltimore: Johns Hopkins University Press, 1975.

Tucker, Robert C. *The Soviet Mind*. New York: W.W. Norton, 1971.

Ulam, Adam B. *Expansion and Coexistence: Soviet Foreign Policy, 1917 to 1973*. New York: Holt, Rinehart & Winston, 1974.

THE AUTHORS

KENDALL E. BAILES is Dean of Humanities and Professor of History at the University of California at Irvine. His book, *Technology and Society Under Lenin and Stalin*, won the Adams Prize of the American Historical Association for 1979. He continues to work in the field of Russian science and culture.

COIT D. BLACKER is Acting Associate Professor of Political Science at Stanford University and Associate Director of Stanford's Center for International Security and Arms Control. He has published widely on Soviet military affairs, strategic doctrine, and problems of arms control.

GEORGE W. BRESLAUER is Associate Professor of Political Science at the University of California at Berkeley and has been Chairman of the Berkeley-Stanford Program on Soviet International Behavior since it began in 1983. He is the author of, among other works, *Khrushchev and Brezhnev as Leaders: Building Authority in Soviet Politics* (1982).

TIMOTHY J. COLTON is Professor of Political Science and Director of the Center for Russian and East European Studies at the University of Toronto. He is the author of *Commissars, Commanders, and Civilian Authority: The Structure of Soviet Military Politics* (1979) and *The Dilemma of Reform in the Soviet Union* (1984).

ROBERT CONQUEST is Senior Research Fellow at the Hoover Institution. Historian, poet, critic, novelist, and journalist, he has written numerous works on Soviet politics and culture, including *The Great Terror* and *Power and Policy in the USSR*.

ALEXANDER DALLIN is Professor of History and Political Science at Stanford University and Director of Stanford's Center for Russian and East European Studies. The author of a number of books and articles on the Soviet Union and international relations, he is currently President of the American Association for the Advancement of Slavic Studies.

GREGORY FREIDIN is Associate Professor in Stanford's Department of Slavic Languages and Literatures. He is the author of a forthcoming study of the poet Osip Mandelshtam, *A Coat of Many Colors*, and of several studies of modern Russian literature.

GAIL W. LAPIDUS is Associate Professor of Political Science at the University of California in Berkeley and has been Chair of the Center for Slavic and East European Studies there. She is the author of books and articles on Soviet society, Soviet women, Soviet nationality policies, and Soviet politics.

MARIE LAVIGNE is Professor of Economics at the University of Paris I (Pantheon-Sorbonne) and Director of the Center for International Economics of Socialist Countries. She is the author of several books and other studies on the Soviet and East European economies.

CONDOLEEZZA RICE is Assistant Professor of Political Science and Assistant Director of the Center for International Security and Arms Control at Stanford. The author of *The Politics of Client Command: Party-Military Relations in Czechoslovakia* (1985), she specializes in comparative civil-military relations and international security problems.

CREDITS

We thank the following for the use of the illustrations that enrich this book:

Pages 42 (A. Kokorekin), 106 (V. Lebedev), 120 (V. Kulagina). *Political Posters*, Aurora Art Publishers, Leningrad.

Page 50. Cartoon reprinted by permission of *The Economist*.

Pages 60 (Vladimir Krinsky), 84 (Alexander Rodchenko). Simon Bojko, *New Graphic Design in Revolutionary Russia*. Lund Humphries Ltd., London.

Page 78. Cartoon reprinted by permission of Doug Marlette, *The Charlotte Observer*.

Pages 94, 138. Poster Collection, Hoover Institution Archives.

Pages 99, 161. Cartoons reprinted by permission of the Tribune Media Services Inc.

Page 103. Cartoon reprinted by permission of the *Albuquerque Journal*.

Page 133. Cartoon reprinted by permission of the Times-Picayune Publishing Corporation.

Page 145. Cartoon reprinted by permission of the *Dallas Times-Herald*.

All works by El Lissitzky are in the public domain.

From the Editors:

We are grateful to all those who made this book possible. We would like to extend special thanks to Jenee Zenger, director of the Stanford Summer College, for her skillful efforts in bringing the authors together for this stimulating event. We appreciate the assistance of the staff of *The Portable Stanford* in making the arrangements for publication and assisting us with the editorial process. Above all, we want to thank our authors who, given an impossible schedule, came through admirably.

THE PORTABLE STANFORD

This is a volume in The Portable Stanford, a subscription book series published by the Stanford Alumni Association. Portable Stanford subscribers receive each new Portable Stanford volume on approval. Books may also be ordered from the following list.

Human Sexuality: Sense and Nonsense by Herant Katchadourian, M.D.
Some Must Watch While Some Must Sleep by William E. Dement, M.D.
Is Man Incomprehensible to Man? by Philip H. Rhinelander
Conceptual Blockbusting by James L. Adams
The Galactic Club: Intelligent Life in Outer Space by Ronald Bracewell
The Anxious Economy by Ezra Solomon
Murder and Madness by Donald T. Lunde, M.D.
Challengers to Capitalism: Marx, Lenin, and Mao by John G. Gurley
An Incomplete Guide to the Future by Willis W. Harman
America: The View from Europe by J. Martin Evans
The World That Could Be by Robert C. North
Law Without Lawyers: A Comparative View of Law in China and the United States by Victor H. Li
Tales of an Old Ocean by Tjeerd van Andel
Economic Policy Beyond the Headlines by George P. Shultz and Kenneth W. Dam
The American Way of Life Need Not Be Hazardous to Your Health by John W. Farquhar, M.D.
Worlds Into Words: Understanding Modern Poems by Diane Wood Middlebrook
The Politics of Contraception by Carl Djerassi
The Touch of Time: Myth, Memory, and the Self by Albert J. Guerard
Mirror and Mirage: Fiction by Nineteen edited by Albert J. Guerard
Insiders and Outliers: A Procession of Frenchmen by Gordon Wright
The Age of Television by Martin Esslin
Beyond the Turning Point: The U.S. Economy in the 1980s by Ezra Solomon
Cosmic Horizons: Understanding the Universe by Robert V. Wagoner and Donald W. Goldsmith
Challenges to Communism by John G. Gurley
The Musical Experience: Sound, Movement, and Arrival by Leonard G. Ratner
On Nineteen Eighty-Four edited by Peter Stansky
Terra Non Firma: Understanding and Preparing for Earthquakes by James M. Gere and Haresh C. Shah
Matters of Life and Death: Risks vs. Benefits of Medical Care by Eugene D. Robin, M.D.
Who Controls Our Schools? American Values in Conflict by Michael W. Kirst
Panic: Facing Fears, Phobias, and Anxiety by Stewart Agras, M.D.
Hormones: The Messengers of Life by Lawrence Crapo, M.D.

Series Editor: Miriam Miller
Production Coordinator: Susan Krever
Cover and Book Design: Andrew Danish

To order additional copies of this book or to add your name to The Portable Stanford subscriber list, just return this postage-paid card.

☐ Please send me _____ copy(ies) of THE GORBACHEV ERA at $9.95 each (California residents add .70 tax). Price includes shippping and handling.

Mr./Ms. _____

Address _____

City _____ State _____ Zip _____

☐ Please send _____ gift copy(ies) with gift card to:

Mr./Ms. _____

Address _____

City _____ State _____ Zip _____

☐ Payment enclosed.   ☐ Bill my Visa/MasterCard (circle one).

acct. # _____ exp. date _____
Price subject to change.

☐ Add my name to The Portable Stanford subscriber list. (Each new book will be sent on approval.)
☐ Please send me the following Portable Stanford volume(s): _____

_____

See back order card for prices (California residents add 7% tax). Price includes shipping and handling.

☐ Please send me _____ PS book bag(s) at $9.95 each (California residents add .70 tax). This includes shipping and handling.

Mr./Ms. _____

Address _____

City _____ State _____ Zip _____

☐ Payment enclosed.   ☐ Bill my Visa/MasterCard (circle one)

acct. # _____ exp. date _____
Price subject to change.

BUSINESS REPLY MAIL
FIRST CLASS   PERMIT NO. 67   PALO ALTO, CA

POSTAGE WILL BE PAID BY ADDRESSEE

The Portable Stanford
Stanford Alumni Association
Bowman Alumni House
Stanford, CA 94305

BUSINESS REPLY MAIL
FIRST CLASS   PERMIT NO. 67   PALO ALTO, CA

POSTAGE WILL BE PAID BY ADDRESSEE

The Portable Stanford
Stanford Alumni Association
Bowman Alumni House
Stanford, CA 94305